Comments from Readers

"One of the best books I have ever read. I laughed, I cried, and I enjoyed every second of reading this book. Thank you to the author."

Ashley RN

"12/10 recommend. A great collection of stories that shows some of the misadventures of those working in the emergency room, but also gives a glimpse to some of the troubles that medical professionals deal with as well. A definite must read."

Joe A

"This is an incredible book. Very well written and everything you have ever wanted to know about the life of an ER doctor. I could not put it down once I started reading it. I would highly recommend this book to everyone. Great read."

Becky L.

"I laughed. I cried. I cringed. I laughed some more. These stories were told in such a way that you really felt like you were there. Excellent job, Dr. McAnonymous!"

Erin RN

"I don't know who this Dr. McAnonymous is, but as an Emergency Department employee I feel as if I have lived every one of these stories in one way or another. This book is the perfect balance of humor, wisdom, and insight. I binged this like it was the latest top ten release on Netflix. I would definitely recommend this book for anyone that works in emergency medicine or healthcare...or those that love medical dramedy. (You know the type,they are drawn to it just like true crime junkies that can't resist a serial killer story.) A good time and a great read. I can't wait to see what Dr. McAnonymous comes out with next!"

Miranda EMT-P, NREMT-P

The Lady Whose Mouth I Set on Fire ... True Tales from the ER

By

Dr. McAnonymous

Copyright © 2020 by Katydid Books

All rights reserved. In accordance with the U.S. Copyright Act of 1976, the scanning, uploading, and electronic sharing of any part of this book without the permission of the publisher constitute unlawful piracy and theft of the author's intellectual property. If you would like to use material from the book (other than for review purposes), prior written permission must be obtained by contacting the publisher at katydidbooks@gmail.com. Thank you for your support of the author's rights.

Cover Illustration, Book Design: Daniel McAnonymous

First edition: January 2021

ISBN 978-1-7355751-3-1

Disclaimer: The content of this book does not constitute medical advice or peer-reviewed training material. The author and publisher are released from any liability for any information in this book.

If only the best birds sang, the woods would be silent.
— Henry Van Dyke (truncated slightly)

Contents

INTRODUCTION

(That does not mean you should skip it)

The Lady Whose Mouth I Set on Fire

I recognized her and she recognized me. I had seen this young woman once before as a patient. She was pleasant, well-mannered and worked as a waitress. Whatever I had seen her for in the past wasn't serious and things must have gone well enough, because she did not act disappointed when she saw me.

She was more mature than most young women her age, made so by the serious disease she had been confronting her entire life. She had one of the bleeding disorders, and on her prior ED trip, I had helped her with administering the medications to stop some bleeding from an injury.

Patients with these afflictions are almost always very well informed. *Medical Pearl: Do not try to bluff and act more knowledgeable than you are around them!* They usually bring their own medications with them, so our job is frequently just to assist them by gaining IV access and deciding how serious the bleeding is (this determines treatment dosages.)

The woman was coming to the ER this time because she had bitten the side of her tongue and it would not stop bleeding. She had been tasting blood for hours. Nothing life-threatening, but seriously annoying.

The bleeding would not stop on its own, but neither of us wanted to use her expensive medications for such a trivial-seeming wound. The goodwill accrued to me from her prior visit was going to be helpful, because I had a plan that I needed to sell to her.

"How about you stick your tongue way out, we spray some numbing medicine on your tongue, and use a cautery stick to stop the bleeding? It won't hurt but a little, and should be quick."

She consented, happy not to need an IV.

I grabbed the bottle of ethylene chloride topical anesthetic. There was usually a bottle of this in the doctor's cubicle. The first task was to make sure it was not empty. This stuff went fast, partly due to playful staff squirting it on each other for laughs. (I never did this.)

The liquid was in a blue-labeled, brown glass bottle that you utilized by holding it upside down, pulling a lever, and directing a freezing, numbing spray on the skin. (This works well for numbing skin for things that are quick and not too painful, like puncturing the thin skin of a ripe abscess.)

The nurse went to get the silver nitrate sticks for cautery. These are like long Q-tips, but with a caustic brown tip instead of cotton.

"I couldn't find the sticks, will this work?" The nurse held up a battery-powered cautery.

"Sure."

As instructed, the patient stuck out her tongue, which I grasped with some gauze for grip and blotted the small trickle of blood.

I pulled her tongue out a little further for access and sprayed the numbing liquid on the bloody area for a couple of seconds. I had to work fast, because the numbing effect is fleeting.

I quickly put down the bottle as the nurse handed me the cautery and I pushed the button. Just before the orange-glowing cautery tip reached the wound, a gentle puff of warm blue fire poofed back in my face. The gauze flared up in yellow as I released her tongue. The mouth glowed with a soft blue flame.

"That's not gonna work," I said matter-of-factly as I discreetly snuffed out the burning gauze. The flaming, wide-open mouth extinguished itself.

I was in full self-control mode. I was the sound of one hand clapping.

Not the nurse—she was the sound of something like, "Oh, my word!"

The patient followed the nurse's lead, not mine, and gasped in mild shock. Any hopes of the fire going unnoticed flickered away.

I hear you, but it *is* possible the smell of smoldering gauze would have escaped the patient.

Closer examination of the ethylene chloride bottle showed a small red "flammable" symbol hidden on the corner of the benign blue label. Some part of my brain knew that, since it was a volatile chemical, but that part didn't speak up in time.

Oh well, the tongue was still bleeding. Time for damage control.

In fact, I was able to smooth things over enough to convince the patient to let me try again when we finally found some cautery sticks. I could tell she was having to steel herself this time.

The second attempt worked fine, with no drama, and the bleeding stopped. Everybody was happy ... but were they?

The ED was giving surveys to exiting patients at the time. I was relieved to see that she had given us the best ratings and wrote no complaints. I was still half expecting a later report of, "I can't taste food," or "I can't kiss my husband anymore," but there were no complaints.

I needed to tell you about the lady whose mouth I set on fire. That's why I wrote this book. But first, I must explain some things. I really did start a fire in a patient's mouth. It is a true story. There are many others in this book.

Every single story in this book is true. I am not going to lie to you.

"Wait just a minute," the wary reader may say.

What's the problem? It's the line, "I am not going to lie to you."

If you ever hear this statement declared in the emergency department of a hospital, it will always be followed by a lie. It is typically an earnest response to certain questions asked of patients: "How much did you drink? Any street drugs?"

"Two beers" means at least double that.

"No street drugs" means cocaine and marijuana.

"Absolutely no drugs" means marijuana.

The emergency department is awash with such lies, and every claim should be viewed with suspicion.

The intoxicated patients typically are the source of lies, but falsehoods can come from any direction. Sometimes, they come from sober doctors: "Tell the police you called me for an emergency! They stopped me for speeding, and I told them the ED[1] called me. I think they are still behind me," said the furtive-looking plastic surgeon.

After a brief pause for processing, I responded: "What? I'm not going to lie to the police! That's probably a felony."

Fortunately, the police never came, and I was not faced with any future unpleasantness from the law or the plastic surgeon (depending on which path I chose).

A similar lie came through the same doors when a different doctor tried the same evasive, *faux* emergency maneuver. In his case, according to reliable sources, the wily police followed Dr. Fugitive upstairs, the nurses chose the "not lie" path, and the doctor was arrested.

---

[1] Emergency Department. Newspeak for ER, Emergency Room, which is regarded as belittling and misleading.

Clearly, lies can cause you problems. Indeed, truth should be the default and is often your only reasonable option. Truth in this book is important to me for several reasons: I want you to believe the stories fully, I do not want to teach any young medical minds anything untrue, and I am trying to reach my own Truth.

So, when I say, "I'm not going to lie to you," I am definitely telling you the truth. But you will need a little more than that. This is what I mean: This book is full of true tales from my life in the ED. Many of them do not sound like they could possibly be true, but they all are. They are not even embellished.

I am going to tell events and facts that I am sure I can distinctly and correctly recall and describe. Yet, in truth, the truth needs some qualifications.

For privacy, legal, and even compassionate reasons, I cannot reveal the identities of the individuals involved. Some of the personal details I have forgotten, and that makes the concealment of their identities easy for me, but that is frequently not the case.

If I give a hair color, then I remember one. For example, "curly blond hair" means I recall the color. This color hair is important, as it was present in both a sad story and a happy one: a young lady mauled to death by a dog, and a young man who miraculously survived death. The narratives are completely true, but the hair color is fake.

I cannot clearly remember the hair color of the girl whose mouth I set on fire, so I did not mention one. I will not guess or invent one for the sake of the story's flow.

I clearly recall the names of both fugitive doctors involved in the events above, so I could mention them, but I will not. For now.

Nothing has been added to the events to make them more scary, yucky, or funny. Everything is true. I am not going to lie to you.

Sometimes I will mention a particular detail because, for some reason, I specifically recall that. I seem to have an unhelpful knack for remembering the less important details. Note that this characteristic of my memory was at times very annoying on important tests in medical school—I remembered exactly where in the textbook the answer is, but not the answer itself.

So, when I write "4A," it means I remember what room the patient was in. I specifically recall that detail because killing a patient sharpens the memory, even if was not exactly your fault and even if the patient was dead only temporarily.

In this book, the quoted conversations may not be word for word, but they will be very close. There will be nothing added of any significance. The most striking of these talks *are* word for word.

None of the names in this book are real. I, Dr. McAnonymous, have changed them all, including my own. It may surprise you to learn that Dr. McAnonymous is not my real name. If you thought it was, this book may not be for you.

Other details could possibly reveal identities, and I have had to change those. Typically, when I mention a descriptive detail or number or name, it is because I remember the actual detail and feel the need to change this for privacy reasons.

To clarify the ground rules and beat the dead horse: all of these stories are true. I will change any details which could be used to identify individuals but none of these changes will materially affect the *trueness* of the stories. In some cases, I will just leave out data, in others, I will change any detail that could give a nosy person some sort of clue. In the plane crash story, I have changed the numbers of the victims involved as an extra precaution.

I have preserved the relevant information in such a way that all of these tales will be recognized by coworkers who experienced them with me.

Do not worry about these modifications. They will not cause you to miss any of the insights these events may contain. You can trust any insight, horror, or laughter you experience here to be a valid response to the real world. The main goal of this book is to relay a reality I have experienced.

When I say "I," the story is my eyewitness account. I am the real doctor. For example, in the story of the lady's mouth I set on fire, the "I" is absolutely me, Dr. McAnonymous.

Can you trust my memory? Some of these tales I recall so precisely because I have retold them hundreds of times over the decades. Many of these events are extremely easy to remember. You will see.

Now that you've suffered through all that methodology, should you even be reading this book?

Anyone planning on treating sick patients should read this book. You need to know what you are getting into. My career is not exceptional, and every experienced ED caregiver will have similar stories. You can fully expect to have your own. Many of your stories will be better, more horrific, funnier, or more shocking. Write them down for the rest of us.

If you are a medical student, you will learn a lot. But if looking for help with your board questions, you are out of luck. With solemnity, I was told in medical school, "Half of what you learn will be obsolete in five years." Well, I learned the wrong half, and now it's all obsolete. Feel free to laugh or gasp at some of the things we did back in the olden days.

I've certainly forgotten way more than I'll ever know, but most of it wasn't important. Much of the information in those gatekeeping classes was just to give the excuse for tests, to weed out those deemed not scholarly enough for medicine.

However, medical student, do not despair.[2] I have written this book for you, really. There is lots for you here. And it is

---

[2] Regarding this book, I mean. Otherwise ...

slightly possible that some snapshot of pathology will help you pass some test or, less likely, impress a nurse. I don't really include any stories about luxatio erecta[3] patients, but I have seen two such cases.

In one of the patients, the triage nurse was fooled into thinking the patient was faking because of the weird appearance of this shoulder dislocation—he looked just like a student raising a hand with a stupid question (no offense). Knowing about this condition would give you the rare chance to one-up a nurse. You may learn some other valuable oddities in this book.

Speaking of nurses, and I obviously always do this with caution (nurses can strike from a distance of more than twice their body length), this book will be perfect for you. You will not learn much, but you will be entertained.

Nurses feel no need to pause at the border checkpoints of civilization, so you may find the verbiage tame, the gore underwhelming, and the jokes lame. If you are looking for the grittiest fare, find something written by a fellow nurse.

One last note. I am telling these stories in the manner I would use when speaking with any student involved with patients. I will mention many things that are not usually mentioned in polite society. Some episodes require anatomic descriptions and I refuse to use the term "down there." Some stories involve gore, death, grieving, etc., and many readers may find the unpleasantness too hard.

Medicine is not for the squeamish. My tone might offend some, but there is no malice or insensitivity here. If you want to help the truly ill, you will have to at least act like you have a ruthless streak, especially in the really hard cases where you have to do painful or invasive things to people. It is not possible

[3] Even most doctors don't know this word. I was taught it by Dr. Google. It is a type of dislocation where the patient cannot lower his or her arm.

to concentrate, to do your job, to save lives if you are too emotional. You cannot intubate and save the dying baby if you have tears in your eyes.

With some fear and trembling, I also recommend this book to any non-medical reader who is interested in seeing the full range of the human experience. This reader needs to not be squeamish or easily offended. There is true horror here. You can turn the page and plummet right into Hell. This is your warning.

My reality has cost me some sleep and given me some nightmares, and the stories herein may do the same to you. Nervous laughs are often the result when I tell these stories, and my wife sometimes winces when I talk. This book may mess you up.

In some way, I feel like we in the medical profession owe it to our patients to record and read these stories. A lot of suffering, pain, and death went into the making of them, and it doesn't seem right for humanity to not have some record of these events. Someone hurt enough that we should resist the blindness that forgetfulness brings.

Whose vision is better? Who sees more clearly? My friends who live in cleaner, brighter, happier worlds, or those of us who are denizens of the dark? To find your way in the ER, your eyes must be prepared for the lack of light.

Unless there is some light, of course, which reminds me of that woman and the mouth fire.

We might as well have started with that story. I am not proud of this episode and I am always embarrassed by telling it, but it has to be told. If just one person learns from my ways, and doesn't follow them, the world will be a better place.

Do not do much of what I have done and recorded here. I list lots of mistakes. The mouth fire story illustrates one type of error. These are the worst: When some part of my brain "knows" the answer but doesn't speak up to convince me of the correct decision when there's still opportunity to get it right.

For example, I might hear a barely audible whisper of, "That's flammable" or "Don't discharge that patient with chest pain," but it just isn't loud enough to override the dissenting parties.

Typically, the correct voice doesn't make itself heard until several hours after the event, when I'm trying to sleep. Then it is very loud and seems unquestionably right. If that voice proves to be correct, then it taunts, "I told you so." Or, "I told you, volatiles are flammable!"

In addition, the mouth-fire incident illustrates the fact that maintaining composure is an important patient care technique. I am fairly certain that nothing in my face or voice conveyed the sudden shock I received when the blue flame burst forth, but that is only because I am in the Zone of Initial Response Control. Any shock on my part might increase her discomfort, adding fuel to the fire, so to speak.

Learn to live in this Zone, because control over your facial expressions or immediate verbal reactions makes a lot of interactions much easier in the ED. Most of your plans will be worthless if you can't get the patient to go along with them. Crinkling your nose at a horrible smell, a micro-expression of anger, a look of condescension, a sudden "Yuck"—all of those things can wreak havoc on your treatment of an ED patient.

In this book, I will insert some pearls and pointers about mastering your initial reactions to sudden surprises, shocks, smells and sights, but first I should tell you about the grain of salt you should be looking for in my advice: I may not be normal.

I feel fine, but that is often not a good indicator. I may have been damaged enough by the events I describe here that my advice is inapplicable to you. I don't think so, of course, so I think you should listen to me, but . . . anyone would be changed somewhat when confronted with these events.

The next chapter marks the beginning of my career, and it may have shaped my whole approach to medicine, and that is part of the reason I want to relate it up front.

In my mind, there is a deadly earnestness underlying everything related to medicine. It should be recognized that all the joking and superficialities float on the surface of a dark, threatening ocean. Some of these stories are funny, *seriously* funny.

I want readers of this book to see the black depths of that ocean first—then, as the eyes adjust, begin picking out the glowing, outrageous, beautiful creatures surviving there.

This whole book exists on the border of life and death, light and dark. The stories are often hilarious, but often sad. The ED does not allow you to have either kind alone. These two regions are pushed into view, both of them forcing you to pay attention.

I apologize in advance if it is too much. It is not overly sad, but it may be overly dark or gory. I cannot really tell. I just know it really happened and it must mean something. It must provide some insight that helps. It is an indispensable part of my life.

This next story is lodged in my brain surrounded by therapeutic, poetical musings, and I will add some of those. I'm sorry if you find them weird. The next chapter tells a horrible, gory story. I do not exactly advise reading it, but I can't help telling it. It is part of me.

1

Planes

I told the story of the lady's mouth I set on fire in the introduction. Wait, did you skip the introduction? Of course you did. Go back and read it now because that may be the best part of the book.

About the mouth fire, that story does not lay heavy on my heart. There were no bad outcomes, and it is mildly humorous. This first chapter is different. Readers may need some preparation, according to my wife.

Do not worry, the whole book will not be like this distressing tale. The other stories I will relate are funny, or medically remarkable; but only sometimes tragic. I chuckled inside while writing the majority of them. I got tears in my eyes recounting a couple of them. I actually cried retelling only one.

But I did not cry when I wrote out this plane-crash tale. Is not being moved to tears a sign of a problem, of some malfunction in my psyche? Has the story lost some of its power because I've told it to myself so many times?

I think it is most likely that the experience is so far removed from human life that I cannot emotionally relate to it, and that any other human being would respond as I have. Sadness—an emotion designed for everyday tragedy—isn't the right label for what I feel.

Numbness and confusion and revulsion and horror and wonder is what I think I feel. I add wonder to the list because the event raises questions for me that seem larger than life: universal, about being itself. The whole episode strikes me as less of a certain chain of events or images; it feels like *the question.*

Plane Crash on Lilac Mountain

Life is a vapor. But so are the clouds that water our crops and make sunsets beautiful. Ephemeral does not mean meaningless. Numinous does not mean without substance.

In my quest for knowledge, I had the idea to ride with EMS[4] workers in an ambulance one morning. In retrospect, the plane crash made that seem like a bad idea.

The day started out well enough, with a nice ride to a school for a little show and tell while we were biding time until a 911 call came.

Lots of laughing children were barely able to control their glee, gawking at the flashy red ambulance and two bright blue uniforms, shiny plastic and metal. Lots of nooks and crannies.

All fun and games for the children, who didn't see what I saw there—tubes to protect airways, pads to shock hearts, IVs to replace blood loss. For this outing, I was not a participant, just a spectator of a happy scene: a little education and a lot of play.

These things can never last long. The children grow up and leave town, the teachers retire and fade from view . . . or things can change a lot more quickly. We got our 911 call.

"Plane crash on Lilac Mountain!"

Here we go. I wasn't expecting exactly that.

The children did not notice the smoke rising north of town. We waved our quick goodbyes as we started off toward the dark billows. I was beginning to get apprehensive. I could get in over my head with multiple trauma victims. Would I have help?

It sounds bad, but I was somewhat relieved when the radio chatter confirmed this was to be a body-recovery call. The thought of treating badly damaged patients in the woods was

---

[4] Emergency Medical Services. Shorthand for the paramedics, emergency medical technicians, and other confusing entities.

terrifying. With no expectation of survivors, we would not be speeding along with sirens blaring (the children would have liked that departure).

It ended up taking a long time to navigate the roads as they deteriorated from paved highway to byway to gravel road to a two-rut track to the base of the mountain, catching occasional glimpses of the smoke rising up, joining and mixing with the grey fog that shrouded the mountains.

Energized and focused deputies took us to the top of the mountain on ATVs or four-wheel-drive vehicles. They were moving with speed and purpose, unusually quiet, no backslapping, no jokes. At the top, we were met by a handful of serious-faced, official-looking men. A tall man who looked very solemn stepped forward and singled me out.

"You're a physician?"

I told him I was, and he asked for no further details.

Someone may have told him about me, but he may have guessed from my appearance—an out-of-place doctor with my white coat, Rockport dress shoes, khakis, tie, and dress shirt. Almost everyone else there was in some type of uniform.

It turned out that the man who approached me was with the Federal Aviation Administration and in charge here. He designated me, the only physician present, to coordinate collecting the remains and assembling them as bodies. He told me that there were nine men and two women, and to do the best I could.

I could do this; I couldn't make them worse.

Medical school is pretty good preparation for most things that can come your way. I had dissected cadavers, attended autopsies, and assisted with amputations. I was now a second-year family practice resident. My license was less than a year old. I was not much of a doctor yet, but still I took on this responsibility without much misgiving.

I *was* a little nervous when I saw the site itself: the multiple scattered small fires, the smoke and diesel smell. But I put this aside, as I was serious about the mission given me. I thought there may be some importance to my task being done well for someone's reputation, since my dad was a professional pilot. He was always annoyed by the tendencies of these investigations to unfairly blame airmen.

Capable personnel strung ropes down the mountainside, and we used them to help us slip and slide to the crash site. My slickish Rockport shoes were not much help, and I wished for my hiking boots at home. The ropes were also necessary to haul up body bags, which we did until one a.m. that night. It was grueling work in a place of horror.

Bare trees in winter, with low grey clouds darkened in areas by smoke. Smoldering brush and flames scattered over the mountainside, like a topsy-turvy hell diving headlong from above, splattering against the ground. The smell of burning fuel, forest, and flesh. Cold-dead leaves no longer crisp, but silently damp with dew, diesel, and blood. Dripping sheets of skin hang from bare tree limbs.

At first, we followed our eyes to lead us to the largest human pieces, but we soon found that we had to pursue a more systematic search because the remains were so scattered. You might see a shirt but find it to be empty, only stains remaining—or maybe it contained a shoulder. I saw the pelvic portion of a torso wedged in the crotch of a tree, covered by a short section of dress pants, belt in place. Momentum carried the rest of the body away.

There were several of these torsos, and they were the largest pieces left. On the ground, we found faces that were masks of skin, with flawless mustaches or eyebrows intact, but nothing to hold their shape. No skulls were intact.

We could feel the cold of the faces through our gloves as they draped over our hands when we placed them in the body bags.

Almost every leaf or tree limb was spotted with diesel, blood, and fat. Twisted bare aluminum, painted metal, fabric, and wire were scattered about, chunks of the jet reduced to a size so small that each could be carried by a single person.

The stunted, bare trees of the rocky slope filtered the bodies through their limbs as they came hurtling down. These wooden limbs, some less than three inches in diameter, were still stronger than the human bone. Shredded fabric and skin hung garishly, red staining everything. We plucked the cold sheets of skin from the branches and sorted them into bags.

We used skin color, hair color, and fabric detail to help decide which bag to place the remains in. Everyone was doing this with some solemnity, I think due less to respect, and more to a stunned numbness.

A pretty female foot, pink toenails perfect, obscured by a shred of nylon stocking, ended abruptly where the ankle should have attached. The plane's occupants had not been blown to "bits," as the saying goes. Things were large enough to be recognized and named.

I could recognize the shiny white head of a femur, a cervical vertebra, liver tissue, a biceps attached to a piece of radius, kidney tissue, etc. There were no intact organs. The faces or scalps could only be matched to the IDs by hair color. Sometimes parts were held together by clothing.

Matching socks were helpful to match feet, which sometimes could be matched to the correct body. The men were dressed with little variation, so there was a lot of best-guessing done. In many instances, there was some debate, but everyone was kind of in a fog and happy to give me the final vote. I do not recall any intact eyes. We must have not found any, because I think I would still see that image.

The science of anatomy prepared me to reckon with the remains of these human beings. They were dissected, reduced to component parts by mass and kinetic energy. I was familiar with these parts—pictured in books, labeled, measured, and catalogued. As a new doctor, I still remembered anatomy in detail and exhaustively. This systematic knowledge proved to be helpful that day; a structured clarity—a protection against the chaotic insanity pressing from every direction.

But no science helped in finding souls amidst the debris—the victims, or our own. What made them human was only seen in fragments: pictures in wallets, name tags, trimmed hair, painted nails. I looked at those things only briefly, only when necessary, only when I couldn't look away.

At some point early on, when the fires were dying out, a news helicopter hovered overhead, fanning flames back to life in our little hell. We all shouted and shook fists. We said it was because of them restarting the fires, but we were really raging at the cloudy heavens, at God.

All day and into the night, we assembled parts that we decided belonged together, placed those in body bags and, when I thought each puzzle was complete, we hauled ourselves and the bag up the slope, the ropes now also stained with blood.

We ended up filling thirteen body bags, two more than we should have. I did my best, but too many things did not make sense. We could not reassemble the parts into eleven complete corpses.

I was given a ride home by my somber new friends. Many of them were younger than me, and less acquainted with such things. I didn't really try to cheer them up.

What can I say about this experience? Am I scarred? Have I gained or lost through experiencing this, both as a physician and human being? I don't really know. On balance, I think it improved me as a physician slightly, added to my confidence. I performed well enough as a leader that day.

I am less sure whether it has helped me as a human being. I feel like some great secret had been whispered in my ear, but I couldn't quite make out the words.

Soon afterwards, I had nightmares of falling helicopters crashing into me. I thought of the day over and over, and in the medical world, when the time seemed right, I have always blurted out my tale, the open faces of others acting as some purgative.

When describing these events at work to students or coworkers, I will sometimes enter a misty distraction that lingers for a while. I do not recall crying when discussing it, but at other times, alone, I have cried.

Three decades in, while I am awake, the pink toes or sheets of skin sometimes become vivid with just a blink. These images are floating on the surface of my mind, but I can't say what affect it has on me more deeply.

Whenever I see some new horror or sadness, these plane crash memories bubble up to come join whatever new bleakness I feel.

Later in life, I flew over Lilac Mountain on a visit to my son. The plane I was piloting was old, a skin of fabric over a tubular frame. I lingered, circling about, but could see no hint of the crash site. Years of falling leaves had buried the past. Time had done its thing for good and ill. From my height, only a few thousand feet up, the mountain itself was a mere wrinkle in the earth's crust.

The visit over, I took off for home from the little airfield. I banked and looked down. My son's face looked up at me, blank due to my height above the ground. I was struck hard with some wistful mood that lasted for days.

Taller than me for a long time now, I suppose seeing him look up made me remember him as a toddler. I also remembered that same face from a distance when we first left him at college. There is something very lonely about a distant face, when it is not moving closer.

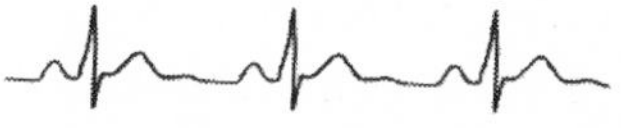

I try not to be the moody type. I believe that too much introspection is harmful. The past survives in our memories and we should put these memories to use, not let them impede the way forward. It is necessary to take steps to keep certain parts of the past from trapping us. For obvious reasons, I approached this crash episode as a potential problem, and while the past was still the present, I'd begun my escape.

So, even while still on that crash scene, I was preparing my mental defense against the psychological onslaught sure to come. There were several thoughts that lessened the tragedy. The plane's occupants certainly felt little pain, if any. Their death was sudden and thorough—no lingering on the edge. Since they just flew into the foggy mountain, they probably had no time to fear the coming death. They were alive, living, not suffering, right until the very end.

I reminded myself of the playing children just down the road. This is life—both these things. Laughing children and death. It is good to surround yourself with the young and healthy. It is also good to keep death in mind.

Fortunately—that needs repeating—fortunately, I did not have to talk to any family members. Now *that* might have been too much. These sudden, accidental deaths are always horrible for families, and giving bad news to these families is a type of horror for physicians, also. For us, there is a world of difference between talking to the survivors of long-sick patients versus the survivors of sudden deaths.

The very old, as well as the very ill, have often considered death for some time. It is no shock to them or their families.

I once informed a very old woman that her husband had just died.

She was gently and lovingly crying, when she said, "I know I shouldn't be crying, he was ninety-five."

This tender, poignant episode is a marked contrast to the sudden wailing or screaming or writhing that accompanies the news of sudden death. I hate this part of my job. The plane crash would have meant enduring this eleven times. I pity the soul who had to tell the families.

Any plane crash is considered news, so decades later, I decided to look it up online. I found pictures of all the passengers, the pilots, and their names. I read the inconclusive FAA reports. I don't think my research was cathartic in any way. The pictures of smiling and elegantly dressed people seemed to have nothing to do with the images in my mind. The juxtaposition only made the lifelessness of the crash site seem alien, unreal.

It is time to take a breath. If you've made it this far, you should read the rest of this book. It's downhill from here. Maybe it's uphill? Whatever, the worst is over with and things will get better, on average.

Keep in mind that this story is a kind of basement beneath all these others to come. Its sadness absorbs the other sadnesses into one dull darkness that exerts constant downward pull. This book will contain numerous hints of an opposing force, small embers of light. In fact, the darker the night, the brighter the stars. Maybe more importantly, you can only see the dimmest stars on the darkest nights.

Wherever this book leads, there is always the weight of a plane crash just north of town acting as an anchor, keeping us positioned to see the seriousness of this whole endeavor.

We see the sparkly sunshine playing on the surface of a creek because of the forces generated by the rocks on the stream bed.

Life and laughter are inherently precious and made even more valuable because they are ephemeral. Life is a vapor—a priceless vapor.

Still, I prefer to be funny and light. I just don't want anyone to think that the lightness can only result from denying reality. I do not want frivolity. Medicine is a big deal. I realize the whole human drama is deadly serious. We all are in a life-and-death struggle; the main difference is the timing.

I don't think laughter has to dull your vision or make you less sensitive to the suffering of others. I do think it is possible to laugh with people, not at them—that is certainly my goal here.

So, life and lives move along. Residency ends, babies come, and I settle into my final career that has now spanned three decades. Like all old doctors, I've treated tens of thousands of patients. Once, I was sworn in as a witness for a case I had treated a couple of years prior.

"Dr. McAnonymous, give us your best estimate of how many patients you have seen," the serious lawyer instructed.

I thought for a few moments and replied, "Thirty thousand."

"Dr. McAnonymous, what can you tell us from your direct recollection about Patient X?" the still-serious lawyer added.

It will not surprise the astute reader that my answer was: "Nothing."

The lawyer did seem surprised, stumbling with the next couple of questions.

Over the rest of my career, I have seen around triple that thirty thousand. Of those tens of thousands of patients, I've only seen two other plane-crash cases. One broke his back in a too-hard landing.

The other one wasn't technically my patient, but I saw him as he rolled to his room. He had crash-landed his little plane, striking a fence. While being rolled to his room, he kept talking on a nonexistent radio, saying things like, "Cessna November 123, turning right base," and "Roger, cleared for landing runway . . ."

Thousands of patients also mean a lot of stress. (I don't have a number for that.) It is often hard to do a good job or keep your wits about you, or even maintain your sanity in the ED environment. De-stressing yourself is one of the best ways to help, and I have learned lots of tricks.

I use one helpful technique all the time to relieve stress. I imagine the worst possible outcome, step by descending step, and come to peace with that (in *theory*, of course). Whatever actually happens is almost always better.

For an example, during a shift, I often am called to do an intubation. I have already thought through this sequence: Intubate normally—fail, try this—fail, try this—fail, call anesthesia—they fail—I attempt cricothyrotomy—fail, patient dies—big-time fail. Lawsuit—lose, house—lose, go live in a tent—OK. I can do that; I can live in a tent. I can be happy with almost nothing.

By doing this, I already have practiced losing everything, and this helps me not to worry. It's like the Olympic gymnast visualizing herself winning yet another gold, only the opposite.

I also will imagine the situation of explaining myself when something goes wrong on a procedure that I had some choice about, say, sedating a child for a certain laceration. The sedation may be the "right" thing to do, but things could go wrong and hindsight must be foreseen.

Something like, "Yes, ladies and gentlemen of the jury, I know she died, but we needed to sedate her because the laceration would have been impossible to sew if she wasn't medicated. She could have been scarred for life."

Always make sure anything you do is reasonable in retrospect, even if everything goes sideways. If it's only a good idea if it works, rethink your options. If you are contemplating some procedure that will increase your stress, at least make sure it is for a good reason.

It should go without saying that prevention is better than treatment. I also try to relieve stress before it occurs. Happy homelife, ritualized preparation for work, pleasant greetings with staff are all helpful before the shift.

Back to the plane crash. I have had several horrendous situations over the years. Once, I directly took care of young siblings who were slashed mercilessly, some to death, others to near death. My partner was taking care of other injured children in this family. It was so horrific for the whole department that the administration held a special dinner and talk for a debriefing. (I had to leave it early to go to work!) It is a shock to me that I cannot remember how many children I took care of. It may have been three. How can you forget such a thing?

I just recall images of little heads with black hair, lots of blood, and chubby bodies with visible fat and muscle. Why isn't there more?

The fact that this mass murder and many other events did not really sear themselves into my memory is, I think, due to the plane crash recalibrating my senses. It is a curse to have to deal with some horrors, but they sometimes give you the blessing of being able to more easily deal with other horrors.

Like the ED, and like I've warned you, this book bounces from light to heavy, from horror to happy, funny to maddening. In the ED, you may treat an infant that dies, then the next patient you see berates you for their wait, hissing, "I don't care" to your explanation. This actually happened to me.

We'll start with a fairly easy bounce to:

The Guy with the Swiss Army Knife in His Head

This middle-aged guy was not sitting still. He got up and down, in bed, out of bed. He was excited, energized, talking a mile a minute. It could have been some street drug, or it could have been the bright red Swiss Army knife stuck into the side of his head. Considering that detail, he was acting pretty normally.

He also had a red mark on his face, the partial outline of a shoe where a concerned citizen had planted their foot in attempts to gain enough leverage to pull out the knife. They were not successful. The skull x-ray was interesting and cheerful, with the little corkscrew and scissors showing up clearly. The knife had penetrated the skull, but just barely.

I telephoned for help. On the other end of the line, the crusty old-school neurosurgeon told me to "ping it out with a hammer."

I was happy to oblige but felt a slightly better approach was to grab the blade with some vise-grips, then ping on that tool, improving the hammer angle and indirectly removing the knife. I was pleased with my plan.

While awaiting maintenance to bring me tools, the neurosurgeon called back. "My son wants to remove it, so we'll be there shortly."

His son was around ten years old. There went my plan. I don't really know which of them removed it, but a CT afterwards showed an insignificant intracranial bleed right at the knife site.

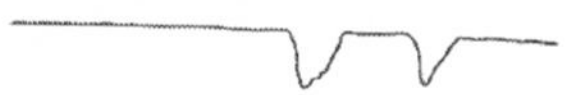

This case and these types of cases are extremely common. They are sort of a lighthearted story combined with potential tragedy. In the "Swiss Army knife to the head" case, the refreshing parts are the patient's attitude, the surgeon doing his thing, and the good outcome.

Now, a child with a cold is also usually a lighthearted case to me and others who are accustomed to living amongst the seriously ill. To add to the fun, these children will frequently burst out laughing at my antics. At this, the mother becomes much less concerned; now she begins to feel relieved. These little kids really cheer me up. In my mind, it is hard for me to even feel they are truly sick, they are just "normal."

To me, sore throats, colds, coughs, sprains—these complaints just prove to me that these patients are healthy. They don't really need *me* much.

The Swiss Army man is more my sweet spot. He does need me, or a surgeon. An even sweeter spot is treating something like a shoulder dislocation—as long as the diagnosis was straightforward, the sedation was smooth, the reduction was successful, and the patient was not hostile. A thankful patient would be gravy, but that is not something you should expect with most patients or meals.

I am satisfied enough even with very ill and complex patients, as long as things go OK. This "OK" can even mean bad outcomes, as long as it's not my fault, I've done good care and the family has been adequately prepared.

Medical Pearl: Be happy with one good patient a day. One "sweet spot" patient where you feel like you are really helping. Do not push too hard trying to make every encounter rewarding.

Bugs in Ears

One of my sweetest spots is treating patients with a bug in their ear. As a fan of inventors, I am proud that I have devised a good way to remove bugs. It works very well on roaches (the most common ear dweller), but I have used it successfully on others, including the very hard-shelled click beetle. Google them.

The click beetle had entered the camper's ear and mostly just napped. It would periodically awaken and do its unique snapping-click maneuver. This snap generates huge g-forces and is the way these beetles escape from predators, suddenly propelling them to safety. My patient did not approve of this behavior in the confines of his ear.

My click beetle man was grown and self-disciplined, so that helped. Younger patients, or the squeamish, are frequently in pain and panicked. Ambulances are called, there is lots of periodic screaming, squirming, and slapping at the ear. Jumping from the bed and trying to run from a bug inside the ear is not unknown behavior. I did have that one calm patient, oblivious to the dead, wax-embalmed roaches in both of her ears, but she was the exception.

Use every trick you know to calm the patient. I don't usually sedate them, because the stakes are low in regard to long-term problems. My technique (not scary) actually helps soothe anxieties. I think the following approach is at least as safe as using the tried-and-true alligator forceps (scary).

My innovation is to use IV tubing connected to suction to remove the bugs. There are variations in these setups, so you'll have to improvise some way to connect the tubing to wall suction. I cut the drip chamber or some other expansion on the tubing to tightly fit inside the suction tube. Then set the continuous suction at a reasonable level. (Test it on your skin. It should make a gentle suction pop when pulled loose—you don't want to remove an ear drum.)

Demonstrate to the patient how soft and unscary the tube is and let them hear it close to the ear. Take the time to get them ready. You will not get many attempts before things get serious. (Escalate to sedation, give up, or send to ENT.)

Under direct visualization, you slide the tubing to the unsuspecting bug's rear end and . . . *thwwittt,* it gets sucked in the tube, and out you pull the bug, half stuck in your tubing, his little legs waving at you (and at the patient, if you dare).

A hiking headlamp and reading glasses for magnification are helpful, if loupes and ENT headlamps are slow in arriving. There are myriads of other techniques that work, but this is my favorite.

Sometimes, as with the click beetle, you have to add some liquid to the ear. This may immobilize the bug if you use lidocaine, but it also helps flush the bug out with the water as you suction. The click beetle came out with the liquid. I didn't even try to get the hard, slippery thing out dry. That would surely have provoked the clicking, and some distress in my patient.

These are nice cases because, ultimately, everyone is happy (except the bug). I occasionally joke about the patient needing to come back when the eggs hatch, but I advise extreme caution in this. Some patients' humor will not be operative in the entomological context.

Since we're talking about bugs, I have to mention one very rewarding activity. This helps de-stress me immensely. First, take one or more patients with a maggot-infected wound. These are only available in season, every year or so. Once all the nurses in the department are on high alert about this patient (thirty minutes to an hour), get some rice. Hospital cafeterias always have rice somewhere—white or brown works.

Place individual, cooked grains of this rice on various surfaces: desktops, computer keyboards, unattended cellphones, arms, shoulders, or hair buns. Let simmer. Enjoy.

It's time for another breath. I considered several possibilities in structuring this book. One of those was a chronological account. I ultimately decided against this idea, but I should relate a few tales from the early days. I will start way back in the last century with medical school. The following is from my time at the VA[5] Hospital.

A Few Training Tales

I was very sleepy in the mornings due to the 100-plus hour weeks. I would walk along the half-mile elevated tube, the human hamster trail, that attached the VA to the rest of the campus. I would slide down the wall, and I am pretty sure I fell asleep as I walked, as each little joint in the railing would periodically jolt me to a brief alertness, a sort of snooze alarm.

I would arrive after my long walk/nap to begin my student duties on the very busy surgery service. How busy were we? We were so busy that we had ten hospitalized abdominal aortic aneurysms at one time, all big enough for surgery, and all big enough to burst.

I can remember inflicting a lot of pain on one old man as I scrubbed his wound daily. I was just following orders as I used a stiff plastic brush to clean off any debris scumming up the surface of the calf-sized wound on his leg, thus making his leg weep blood and his eyes weep tears. My faith in the system stood firm at the time. In retrospect, a more genteel approach to wound care comes to mind.

We were so busy we had to delay removing a doomed foot. The foot could not be saved; but the patient could. We injected a ring of lidocaine at the ankle, tied off the foot with a tourniquet, then froze it solid with dry ice. It was my job the next few days to make sure the foot did not kill the patient by thawing until the more reliable removal was performed.

---

[5] Veterans Administration. At the time, an understaffed and overpatiented place.

One of those time-bomb abdominal aneurysms made it to surgery. This man gained slightly over fifty pounds in the course of one day, in a long, complex abdominal aneurysm and kidney operation. I personally helped weigh the bed pre- and post-op, so this weight gain was no estimate.

After the surgery, I discussed the bloated man with the anesthesiologist and asked, "Wow! How did you keep his electrolytes from going haywire?"

He replied, "We just keep a close eye on them."

Wrong answer! His first lab results all came back strikingly abnormal. My faith swayed a little in the breeze.

This anesthesiologist looked old and wise to me, but that's because I was young. My faith in the system was at least partly based on an illusion, the trappings of truth. Most doctors looked old, authoritative. Nowadays, of course, it's the opposite to me, everyone looks young, the illusion reverses, so I have to trust their training or reasoning or agile minds more.

On other rotations, I can recall a few things. AIDS was a new disease. I obtained a fresh tube of bright red, deadly blood from this poor soul's radial artery every hour all through the night. The team was not going to be caught off guard by hypoxia. This often occurred with the pneumonia commonly found in these patients back then.

I remember staying up all night, syringing ice water in, and pumping it back out of this old man's stomach in obsolete attempts at treating upper gastrointestinal bleeding.

On one rotation, my team received a consult for a "blown pupil" occurring after surgery. The neurology team quickly diagnosed a glass eye as the cause.

That same team was slow to treat a sixteen-year-old girl with obvious meningitis, delaying antibiotics as we fumbled around trying to get the lumbar puncture in a misguidedly academic approach. She would have died anyway, but everyone was distressed that we were not at our best. I can remember the face of the crying first-year resident handling the case. I went with her as she informed the family.

Residency comes next and I could mention more:

There was a huge man, delirious with meningitis, strapped to a bed that he could so violently shake that he and the bed would vibrate around his ICU room, like the little foam players on one of those buzzing electronic football games.

Or the resident who tried to convince the patient to drink the CT contrast by taking a swig himself. The patient was not convinced as the resident threw the foul liquid back up with gusto.

In spite of the warnings above, I do have some wisdom to offer. As for my credentials, I have successfully practiced in an emergency setting for three decades. I have never been successfully sued in this setting. (More on that later and, also a big "Yet.") I have never gotten in major trouble and have not even made any tremendously horrible mistakes. (You will likely disagree if you are the judgey type and may have already reported my burning-mouth story to some authority.)

I also have had a good family life and am retiring upper-middle class. I succeeded in my dreams where others with even more of a head start have not. I think my perspective is worth listening to. A reasonable reader may get tired of my commentary, but if these stories do not interest you, you are not interested in medicine or people. We may as well get started with the most common real trauma, vehicle wrecks.

2

Cars

I won't only talk about cars in this chapter. There are always motorcycles, or "murdercycles."

Cars have gotten notably safer over the years. Gone are the days when almost every wreck was accompanied by lots of suturing, or frequent horrific injuries, like the two nineteen-year-old boys who both became quadriplegics in the same car wreck.

People fare better these days, but the cars fare worse. Of course, that's why car wrecks are safer these days. All these crumpled, crushed, totaled cars sacrifice themselves. The old vehicles were damaged less, but at our bodies' expense. However, motorcycles have increasingly roared in to keep up the carnage.

Medical Pearl: To check the airway, loudly ask the EMS, "Is this the man in the scooter accident?" If you do not hear the patient respond, "It was a motorcycle!", you will likely need an advanced airway.

Motorcycle wrecks have impressive variability. I once saw two couples going zero miles an hour, sitting motionless at a stoplight, twin pairs of retirees on bikes. The truckdriver behind them slipped on his clutch, bumping forward a few feet and *crunch!* All four patients had either one or both legs badly fractured.

Of course, most wrecks occur at speeds much faster than zero miles an hour. I have seen two riders who wrecked when going over 100 mph. One was a teenage girl motorcycle drag racer (You thought soccer was scary, Mom?). She was fully decked out in protective gear and I don't recall a scratch. There may have been some little abrasions, but none that required my attention. The same "non-injuries" were sustained by a motorcycle enthusiast who was trying to speed away from the police. *Note: This type of avoidance behavior is often an early warning sign of traumatic injury.* He was clocked exceeding the magical 100 mph and saved from serious harm by his leathers and pads.

Many of the guys wearing protective riding suits are reciprocally very protective of the suit. We normally just cut the clothes off of any accident victim with serious injury potential, but these riders will sometimes plead the case of their suits loudly and shame us into a lot of extra work carefully cutting seams to allow for future repairs.

This protective gear can only do so much. Once I walked into a trauma room and noticed two motorcycle boots. They both were properly placed on the feet, but one of the feet was not properly placed on the body. It was on the little bedside table.

The foot's owner was riding on the back when the cyclist lost control, briefly making an off-road excursion. This resulted in his girlfriend's leg contacting the signpost, creating a clean, but non-anatomic separation. This became apparent to them both soon, and the boyfriend safely stopped and went back to pick up the girl's leg on the shoulder of the road. EMS brought all three to the ED.

The boyfriend was shaken, the patient was stable, and her boots were undamaged. It looked like things could be made right. However, the several places I called confirmed that even with the almost-perfect conditions for a limb replacement, legs are better off not being reattached.

If this doesn't scare you away from riding on the back of a motorcycle, the next story definitely won't.

The girlfriend had fallen off the back of a wrecking motorcycle. The driving boyfriend broke his arm in the mishap. The girl was not very injured.

The asphalt had sanded away at her, sequentially removing a small circle from her back pockets, blue jeans, panties and skin. She had two perfectly round abrasions, symmetrically placed on either half of her bottom.

"He broke his arm. It's nothing really bad. Your boyfriend will be fine," I reassured.

"You mean my ex-boyfriend," she sneered.

Ouch.

There are lots of painful, but not dangerous abrasions, but motorcycle accidents are not laughing matters. I have seen many deaths or mangled bodies due to them. I suspect they are our largest source of fatal pelvic fractures.

Motorcycles are definitely scary. I saw a guy who had died from a wreck. To add to the tragedy, his wife also saw him die from the wreck, so I wasn't really giving her bad news she didn't already know. She was just behind him in her car and saw the whole thing. She was pitiful. She was a nurse.

Now I don't mean to sell cars short; safety has improved, but they still are responsible for a lot of death and destruction. The next story is not an ED case (it certainly could have been) but at least we're finally making it to car wrecks.

How I Earned My MVA

This tale involves myself and my whole family of four, two adults and two young teens.

We were all packed into my Hyundai Elantra, zipping along I-75 in Tennessee, headed north to Oshkosh, Wisconsin, for the big airshow. We were listening to The Great Course's Bob Greenberg pontificating about music on our CD player.

We were a little grey car leading a line of several others in the slow lane. An eighteen-wheeler was passing all of these, forgetting about our car as he pulled back into our lane.

I felt our tail get gently shoved to the right as we began sliding sideways at seventy-five miles per hour. Chrome and blue towered over the window on my left. Time slowed, accompanied by a realization of *this is it.* An odd quietness. I was fully expecting the Big Crunch any second but hadn't really built up any fear yet.

Still in the bizarre, time-suspended mood, I stated, "I love you K—."

She responded to me with "I love you, too," as she turned off the CD player. Question: Why did she do this? Don't ask me, or her. She has never given an adequate justification.

I reflexively turned the wheel into the slide (I grew up driving on dirt roads.) At that point, I felt the responsiveness of the car and the idea that we may live flashed before my eyes, and I began fighting to recover control. I succeeded partly, fishtailing across the median. "This is just like a bad grass strip landing," I thought as optimism raised his hand in my mind. He quickly jerked the hand back down when we continued sliding, brakes locked, into the oncoming traffic on the other side of the freeway. Fortunately for all, several drivers braked or swerved appropriately, and we spun out to a stop, facing north where everyone else was facing south. Optimism had the right answer after all.

My wreck behavior gained me lots of brownie points from my wife for several reasons: One, I told her I loved her, right before we died. Two, I said it first. Three, I got her name right.

The trucker who hit us stopped a couple hundred yards down the road and walked over to check on us. He was really shaken up. I was fine, maybe a little overly cheerful. My wife was calm, sort of, her usual state. My daughter was talking about seeing the grill of the truck and my son was apparently bored.

The car was not really drivable. The wheels were bent sideways and the entire back half of the driver's side was beat up. There were semicircular lug nut scratches on my daughter's door. The truck driver mentioned looking way down and seeing her look way back up at him.

The trooper let us limp the car back to an exit. The trucking company excitedly urged us to spend for anything we needed. (They said they had a $100K deductible.) I helped the trucker bend his damaged bumper further away from his front tire, and he was headed back north, clearly shaken.

His company encouraged us to rent a nicer car for the rest of the trip, which we did. I was extremely annoyed when the rental car guy who picked us up kept using his phone and steering with his knee with my kids in the car.

We enjoyed the airshow at Oshkosh, although a pilot died when his Mustang was clipped by another landing plane. We were at the other end of the strip so were spared any horrific details. We saw wings roll just above the ground, then a fire. The smoke rose for some time over the somber crowd, but in only a few hours, the decision was announced, and the planes rose again.

On the way back home, we took a detour through a state park. Near the entrance, we ran over an iron grate which clanked loudly, startling us all to an uncomfortable degree. We were definitely a little on edge, but the winding drive through woods and meadows and watching the animals restored us.

On the way out of the park, I saw the grate across the road coming up a few yards ahead.

"Is that a deer?" I gestured to the right, hoping my wife would search intensely. She did, and, as I planned, she was focused outside just as we banged over the grate. I was not startled, but my wife sure was. My fun was spoiled when my wife burst out crying. Too soon. There went those brownie points.

The car was eventually fixed, except for the rear window heater. The trucking company spent $11K on repairs on a $17K new car. None of us occupants needed any repairs that we could see. Yet.

Later, I had one nightmare involving a helicopter crashing into me, which seemed somewhat related psychologically speaking. It is impossible to survive unscathed in this world, mentally or otherwise. It is actually impossible for anyone to survive for long. Time is relative, and our lives are relatively short.

The only other car wreck I have ever been in was when my son and I got struck in the Chevy Cavalier's passenger side by a tow truck carrying a pickup. He "didn't see the stop sign." It was a big, loud explosion from the right, and our momentum spun us around to the other side of the intersection. I noticed the windshield shatter in front of me, then the smoke. Of course, fooled by the airbag debris, I thought the car was on fire and turned to rescue my son, who bore more of the impact. He was already briskly headed my way, so we exited my side together.

I remember two guys in a propane truck who stopped to help. They helped by kicking some roadside beer bottles away from my car's door: "I don't think these are yours, but who knows what the police will think?"

I called my wife, and she came to retrieve us as another tow truck came to retrieve the car. The tow truck that hit us had been disabled by a last-ditch defensive stab from my Cavalier's deformed bumper. That car died trying to save us.

We also retrieved some flowers from the trunk of our car that I had purchased for my wife. More brownie points gained when I handed her these, but quickly lost as I pointed out, "I guess the wreck wouldn't have happened if I hadn't stopped to buy flowers." Too soon, again.

We went to the beach for the next few days and I observed some weirdly patterned bruises on both of us. I performed serial abdominal exams on my son and myself, since we were hit hard enough to damage some things. Nothing bad ever turned up.

I know, I know. Any of you bloodthirsty medical students are now bored. You don't want to hear about me or brownie points.

Just for you, I will now get into some more medically interesting cases.

Assorted Cases

Case 1

I once saw a young girl after a car wreck. She went into cardiac arrest en route from blunt trauma and, like almost all of these cases, it was too late for the ED to help when she was delivered to us. She had subcutaneous air bloating up her entire torso. The air was blown up so tightly under the taught skin, that you could thump her like a drum. She must have transected[6] something big in her airway.

Case 2

I have only sent flowers to one patient's funeral my entire career. This was actually a funeral for two.

We got advance notice that these patients were coming. The rumor mill was grinding so efficiently that we knew it was a car wreck involving the daughter and granddaughter of a well-known nurse who worked in the hospital across town. All these warnings didn't help, because when the patients arrived, it was already too late.

We were doing lots of things: IVs, tubes, blood, more tubes, but nothing was going to work. The victims were a beautiful, young, black-haired toddler and her matching mother. The scene was more emotionally charged than even this horror

---

[6] To cut across. This may seem like unnecessarily jargonish, but it has specific meaning for the poor sucker tasked with repairing such an injury.

would typically be since several of the nurses knew the two patients.

The emotional charging was not over. We were still working in focused futility, when the husband/dad arrived. Overcome with fear and dread and well, everything, he barreled through anything or anyone in his attempts to get to his family in the trauma room, shouting and making a huge disturbance. Since we were still working intensely on both patients, the security guards correctly assumed we did not need to be disturbed.

The distraught father, however, was not to be stopped, and in desperation the security guards pulled Tasers. The shouts from the man as well as those trying to control him were even louder, more primal. He finally stopped at the room door. I looked up to see him on his knees with his hands behind his back, laser light spots playing over his shirt.

It was all a bit much for me. The little girl, the young mother, the father and the grandmother nurse bound us all tightly to the destroyed little family.

I sent flowers to the funeral of the little girl and mother, but I did not go myself.

Actually, this was the first text messaging wreck I treated, with the last text still found on the phone beside the road. The car had run into the back of a log truck.

Case 3

The pelvic x-ray looked fine, with everything symmetrical and no breaks, but the woman did not. She had intense pain with any movement of her legs, pain like a fracture or dislocation. It was a little puzzling until I noticed, "Wait, *both* hips are dislocated."

Case 4

That reminds me of this other guy. He had one of those weird wrecks, one in which he just inexplicably ran into something.

He had the appearance of an upstanding citizen type, and so drugs seemed even more unlikely than alcohol.

We suspected a seizure or heart attack or hypoglycemia, something to make him unconscious and then wreck his car. He did not recall what had happened, and all he noticed now was severe bilateral shoulder pain.

His initial trauma survey was OK, and his limited initial x-rays looked normal. The slightest movement of either arm caused intense pain in his shoulders. I could see intact, normal shoulders on the chest x-ray, so this made me more concerned that something more ominous than broken bones was going on. I was worried that a neck injury or some vascular injury was causing his shoulder pain.

The trauma residents arrived. The patient would clearly need lots of scans and hospital admission. It was the end of my shift, so I turned him over to the trauma service and left. On the way home, that little mousy voice finally broke through, "Bilateral shoulder dislocations from a seizure, not the wreck itself."

I called the hospital and left the message with a resident. I doubt that anyone gave me credit for my pre-scan diagnosis, which was soon noted on the CTs done by the trauma team. Regular x-rays don't always show these dislocations.

The seizure caused the shoulder dislocations, then the wreck. Further workup found that the seizure was caused by a brain tumor. The patient was a neurologist.

Case 5

The middle-aged man had been in a high-speed MVA[7] and was being wheeled into the department, strapped on a backboard. I scrambled along beside him:

---

[7] Motor Vehicle Accident. This terminology is amazingly contentious. Others lobby for Motor Vehicle Collision.

Airway: He was yelling, so that was good. His c-collar[8] was in place and he was secure on the backboard.

Breathing: His lung sounds were equal bilaterally and the chest was rising normally as he took in a breath to scream.

Circulation: He was pale, and I could not feel a radial pulse as we wheeled along to Trauma 6. That was not good.

"It's my hip, my hip!" The screaming took shape in my mind as I slowed to process his words.

"How's your chest, does this hurt?" I asked as I interrupted him and pressed on his chest.

"No, you idiot, it's my hip!"

That interchange summarizes his last few hours of life. As we systematically checked each critical system, asking about any resulting tenderness, his answer always followed the same pattern. He would insult us, then redirect us towards his hip. We all believed him, that his hip was a problem, but it might not be the only or even the worst of his problems.

His insulting behavior evolved in complexity, and he was asking for names and really giving the nurses a hard time as they started IVs, placed monitors, and inserted an assortment of tubes in or about his person in their attempts to treat him.

He ultimately proved right, as we found no other immediately life-threatening injuries. His hip—or more precisely his pelvis—was badly broken.

This man did not go gently into his good night. He may have had no other injuries, but his one big one made him increasingly unstable. His insults never stopped, only diminishing to a whisper, until everything stopped, and he was finally at peace.

The nurses were upset, some in tears: "I was so mad at him, I can't believe he died," was the gist of the talk. They weren't just

---

[8] Cervical Collar. Keeps a potentially broken neck from flopping about. EMS rescue videos from the 50's detail a shocking obliviousness to necks.

crying over the patient, they were crying over themselves, in pain that they could be so provoked to anger by a dying man. I tried to expiate the guilt of their anger with things like, "He was a jerk, nothing changes that. We were doing all we could do for him. You were trying to help, it's OK to be mad *and* sad." I was not much help.

In the not-too-distant past, it was common for patients to die with pelvic fractures, which can bleed massive amounts into the retroperitoneum. We used pelvic binders, an industrial-duty corset to help decrease the bleeding. But at that time, it was not possible to definitively stop pelvic bleeding with today's interventional radiological techniques.

I have seen several patients quietly drift off to death from these fractures. The pain seems to evaporate as the lips grow pale, the patient becomes silent, and soon unresponsive, never to experience pain again.

It appears to me that bleeding to death is one of the better ways to go. You slowly fade into a state where you do not notice the frantic attempts around you. Respiratory deaths seem a lot worse.

Another notable hip story was courtesy of a car wreck:

Case 6

Early in the trauma surveys, I noted a huge gap in the front of his pelvis. His symphysis pubis had a two-finger wide gap that I could easily feel. This man had a low blood pressure, so we quickly applied the pelvic binder.

With this in place, his x-ray looked normal. I was amazed at how effective the binder was, at least visually. It was impossible to see on the x-ray any trace of the fracture I had just felt. Fortunately, the CT showed some fragments here and there about his mostly normal-appearing pelvic bone.

I say "fortunately" because that made it easier to decide to send the unstable patient to IR instead of the OR (spelling counts). I would not like my fingers alone to signal the alarm as this could create some awkward discussions with the surgeons. I was happy to have the CT confirmation of my exam.

The Interventional Radiology team had clogged up the bleeding as planned, but in so doing had to release the pelvic binder. When they called me over to retighten it, I felt the familiar gap at his pubis. I could fit two fingers in a gap where I should fit none. I retightened the binder and the deformity disappeared again. I was hoping all the movement didn't mess up any of IR's life-saving handiwork.

Case 7

I like to practice my very limited Spanish, so I was not troubled by the helicopter EMS report that the patient didn't speak any English. This patient had been in an MVA with the high probability of injury, so a nuanced conversation was not initially important.

As we moved him into the trauma room, various personnel performed the ABCDE's of trauma care, cutting off his clothes, inserting lines, carefully moving him, and so on.

Part of my role was to ask him a few questions and look for specific injuries and complaints. Communication is important, but not absolutely vital, as many of these trauma patients arrive completely unresponsive.

Because of this, my attempts at bilingualism were fine initially. I considered it a challenge. I have gotten good enough that the patients sometimes answer with a flood of verbiage they expect me to follow. Of course, I am left behind. Anyway, in a trauma, my medical Spanish mostly consists of pressing on something and asking if it hurts.

"¿Dolor aqui?"

The whole team laughed at my pronunciation, as my butchery was apparent even to those who knew no Spanish.

I did not mind the laughter because things were going well. With the expanded borders of my verbal skills, I ascertained the patient's position in the car, his allergies, his smoking status, and his areas of pain. "¿No problema respire?" also got me the main answer I needed.

I was particularly proud when he lifted his left leg to my, "Levante los piernes izquierda." At that moment, a real Spanish speaker arrived.

"Hey, can you see if I've got this guy's story straight?" I asked the real-deal bilingualist.

After a few rapid-fire exchanges in Spanish between the interpreter and the patient, the interpreter asked something like, "Habla inglés?"

The patient said, "Yes," without much accent and switched to English. Now the team was definitely laughing at me, not with me.

I weakly offered some head injury hypothesis for the earlier misunderstanding as the nurses all rejoiced together at my humiliation.

Of course, interpreters aren't infallible. One of our bilingual nurses would typically translate the patient's occasional English answers needlessly to English for my benefit, sometimes with a heavier accent than the patient.

Another time, a patient and I were having a three-way conversation with the web-based interpreter. We moved the camera around so we all could be seen and heard, and it worked OK.

At the conclusion, I remarked:

"Wow, I guess you could be anywhere. Mrs. R— and I are stuck here in the hospital, where are you?"

There was a guilty pause. "At the beach."

That would be nice. I guess it's possible I could do that with telemedicine, but at least for now, I like to be at the scene of the crime.

Even if you speak the same language, it doesn't mean you are communicating. EMS reports can sometimes lead you astray. Once, "ambulatory at the scene" meant "took two steps and collapsed" for a badly injured MVA patient. This next case began with "fell from standing."

Case 8

This man was flown in by helicopter with the report of "fell from standing." The patient couldn't elaborate on this. Maybe he hit his head and lost that memory; his mentation was normal enough now.

At first glance, he looked pretty beat-up, with abrasions scattered all over and a dislocated shoulder. I could find nothing else wrong, but he still looked like a trauma case. I ordered the normal trauma stuff, then called the trauma surgeon.

"He fell from standing?" he asked.

"Yes sir, they were clear about it, he just looks like something more happened." My Jedi force was weak in this case.

"Well, McAnon, we can't put a fall-from-standing on the trauma service." I had no real defense (in those days—we have new rules now.)

Not being shocked by his answer, since it was plenty reasonable, I continued plugging along, not finding much beyond the dislocated shoulder, which I happily reduced. A CT of his head was normal, but he still had some amnesia. The multiple abrasions were making him a little hard to evaluate for subtle injuries.

The family arrived, and after a few preliminaries I asked, still having a hard time believing it:

"So, he fell from standing?"

"Yes, he was just standing there, then fell."

Then the family added the punchline:

"Then he bounced off the roof."

Bingo!

Ring, ring: "Umm sir, the family now demystified things by reporting that he fell from standing then adding . . . off of the roof."

"OK, McAnon, I guess we can take that."

3
Guns

The police officer had a large hole in the center of his forehead. It was about a centimeter in diameter and dark red with congealed blood. The officer had been transferred from a hospital about forty-five minutes away. He was sitting up on the EMS stretcher, and that alone was a very good sign, other things considered.

He seemed fine. He was not even particularly nervous at this point. He was oriented, thinking normally, breathing, moving arms and legs. Everything *was* fine, and he was starting to understand that. He smiled intermittently and only admitted to mild pain at the wound site when asked. This was around an hour after he was shot, so things looked pretty positive. I sent him off for a CT scan.

"The wife is here," I was told by the registration clerk.

This will not be bad at all, I thought cheerily. I wouldn't have to worry so much about my face. I am always anxious my expression would highlight the obvious fact that I am not grieving as much as the family.

His wife sat down quickly. She was maybe thirty, distraught, hungry for information, expecting the worst, with smeared mascara from her tearful trip to our place.

"Hey, I'm Dr. McAnonymous. Are you Officer P—'s wife?" I was not carefully solemn. "Yes? Well, your husband is OK for now . . ."

She interrupted: "No, no! He was shot!"

"Yes, I know. I've seen him and he's fully awake, acting normal and ask—"

"No! My husband was shot in the head!"

now, yes. We're talking about the same man."

d etc. This went on for several more exchanges before I finally convinced this poor young lady that her husband was currently fine and asking for her. The bullet went through his skull and lodged between the hemispheres of his brain, causing little problem in the ED or in the future.

Somebody had called 911 and shot the officer through a window when the police arrived. The window, the distance, the particular type of gun, all these things conspired to create this unusual outcome. The large bullet sitting in his brain made the CT images impressive.

He left the department laughing with his wife. I suppose the neurosurgeons went after it, just lying between the two hemispheres. Surely the brain doesn't do well with a bullet rattling around in the skull.

However, contrary to every movie ever made, most bullets are just left in, their presence less risky than any surgery to remove them. This particular bullet seemed to be a reasonable exception to the rule.

It is possible he suffered complications or infections afterwards, but I only have happy feelings associated with this event. I am likely to have heard about him either way, so I think a continued good outcome was most probable.

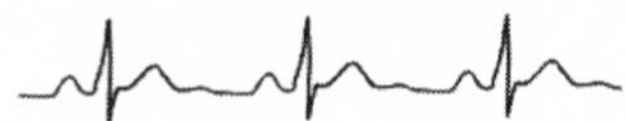

I did not expect a good outcome from the following case. Even if the actual gunshot proved not to be a long-term problem, he had other concerns.

This man came in with the report: "GSW[9] to head, self-inflicted." I walked into the room to see him seated on the side of the bed, bent over with his hands on both temples. He looked like he was staring intently at the floor. But his eyes were held closed, and he was grimacing in some sort of distress.

"Are you OK?" was my first question.

"My head hurts!" He said this emphatically, with a tone strongly conveying that there are stupid questions, and this was one of them.

He had a typical entrance hole in the right temple produced by his 9mm pistol. The rest of the right side of his head appeared normal. The left half of his head was one huge hematoma. The skin was intact but floating off his skull like a water balloon. His CT showed lots of tiny bullet fragments sprinkled along an obvious path through his frontal lobes, and the bullet lodged in the hematoma under the skin on the left side of his head.

Of course, most gunshots to the head are not survivable. One physician in town recounted with horror having to intubate someone who blasted his own face off with a shotgun. I remember two of these similar cases who roamed around my medical school. Their "faces" were flaps of thick skin the plastic surgeons had cleverly repositioned from their backs. I saw one of them smoking through a tiny hole that replaced his mouth. I cannot recall his eyes. He made not have had them.

Most of the gunshot victims that I see in my town survive. I estimate that the ratio is about five to one, nonfatal to fatal. The badly injured but salvageable victims are quickly taken up for repairs by the trauma surgeon. Those on either extreme are more my responsibility.

---

[9] Gunshot Wound. I know, everybody knows that one, but some may be RUI (Reading Under the Influence)

The non-critical GSW victims almost always want the bullet removed, and we almost never comply, although that stance may be changing a little these days.

I remember this guy who had gotten shot in the left upper arm. He and I could feel the bullet bulging beneath the skin of the back of his arm. It had entered through the front. He kept pleading with me to remove the bullet, but I kept trying to convince him of the safety of leaving it alone. Maybe he could convince a surgeon to take it out later, when he had otherwise healed, to minimize complications.

As I was talking and exploring his wound, I noticed some fabric protruding from the entrance hole. I started pulling on this gently, trying to keep it intact. It soon became apparent that it was somehow still connected to the bullet. If I tugged on the cloth sticking out of the wound on the front of his biceps, the bullet got pulled deeper into the back of his arm.

There may have been other, safer courses of action, but these did not occur to me at the time. I slowly twisted the fabric to increase its strength and simultaneously withdrew it, hoping to get as much of the fabric out as possible. The bullet seemed to follow along. I did some testing by pinching the bullet through his skin and pulling some. The connection seemed sturdy. I decided to keep withdrawing and twisting.

Soon, I teased out a long wad of twisted fabric along with the enfolded bullet. I swung this unusual pendant so the patient could see. He was happy the bullet was out. I was happy to send him home without a large swathe of shirt sleeve buried in his arm. That could have caused a huge infection.

Bullets move in mysterious ways. One bullet from a tiny gun might kill you, and six holes from a big gun might do little permanent damage. Of course, even the tiny ones have to be treated.

I once saw a little boy who had been shot in the chest with a pellet rifle. He had a .177 caliber hole in his left anterior chest, right over his heart, but unfortuntely not right over a rib which may have stopped it. He had no complaints and was otherwise normal.

I got the chest x-ray and was a little surprised I couldn't find the projectile. It was not in his abdomen either. You have to look carefully because they can really go unexpected directions. The patient still had no complaints, so I rechecked his chart. EMS reported he had some leg pain during the trip in.

The nonchalant youth shrugged, "Maybe I did, there's no pain now."

An x-ray of his thigh showed the mischievous little pellet. It must have entered his heart or aorta and gotten pushed down into his femoral artery—an embolus of lead. This one couldn't be left in because it might float downstream and block off a pretty big artery or cause other problems.

The vascular surgeon fished it out with a balloon catheter. Other than the small hole, the boy never showed any other sign of chest injury.

Another kid had a pellet stuck right in his forehead. The pellet aspect was nice because that meant there would be a little skirt on one side that would make it easier to grab than the slick, spherical BBs that are also common.

"How did you get shot in the head?" I asked, making small talk.

"I was trying out the bulletproof vest I made," the child said. I maintained an interested appearance, squelching anything that might have seemed inappropriate to the young fellow.

"Who shot you?" I asked, keeping the conversation going.

He motioned behind me, "My dad."

I turned to see a sheepish gentleman, with very thick glasses. As I mentioned earlier, it is important to have control of one's facial expression.

The very littlest guns can do some real damage. Even the low-velocity BB guns of course can cause injuries to the eye. I only recall one BB to the eye. Less serious injuries are more common, and I've rescued lots of the shiny gold "gems" from shallow skin wounds.

The bigger guns are more common producers of patients for us. Intentional shootings, suicides, and accidental discharges are all common. A lot of really bad decisions are made, and these may have disastrous consequences.

I once saw a teen that shot himself in the head with a .38 revolver. Amazingly, he was fine. The bullet entered at a shallow angle, skimmed along the skull, and exited from the top of his head. The skull was intact and there was no apparent injury to his brain.

"I cocked the hammer, and now I knew I had to shoot it to get the hammer back down, and before I know it, blam!"

The bad-decision titer was high in the case of the soldier who shot himself in the hand with his 9mm. He was holding the muzzle hard against his palm trying to prove some point about how this particular gun worked. He made a different point.

His comrades-in-arms tried to be supportive. In responding to my confused questions about semiautomatic pistol functions, one soldier said, "Only an idiot would . . ." then trailed off as he realized he was describing the actions of his injured buddy.

I suspect most firearm wounds I've seen have had serious consequences—either death or life-changing damage. Even the least damaging leaves a big scar. In our small city, there are around a dozen killings a year.

The young guy needed a left-sided chest tube. He was not in good shape, and he was a "scary" patient. He had bad vital signs and a big gunshot hole over his heart. I put the chest tube[10] in without trouble and was seeing blood as I expected. I did not expect *this* volume of blood. It kept coming, and it kept pulsing through the large, clear tube in a regular pattern.

The medical student said, "You're in the heart."

I tried to dismiss this idea as too far-fetched, but the bullet could have made an opening . . .

"You're in the heart!" He kept saying this and got louder with each repetition.

The blood kept regularly pulsing into the tube. Lots of it.

"You're in the heart! Pull it out!"

Now, I was the attending, so I didn't have to follow the student's orders, but he was certainly adding to the anxiety I already felt. I also shared his natural impulse just to quickly pull it back out, but that was not the right action.

The right action was what I "calmly" did. I let the tube do its job, get the blood out of the chest into the cell-saver so we could give it back to the patient in his veins, where it was supposed to be. The pulsations were due to the lung motion pushing the blood out in just such a manner that it simulated a pumping heart.

I put quotes around "calm" because I know I was anything but calm. It was all an act. Acting cool helps you *be* cool when it counts. It doesn't much matter if there's panic somewhere deep, you just have to keep that submerged so you can think straight and act straight.

Interestingly (at least to me), I am most likely to start to leak emotions at the very end of my shift, when the possibility of home and another life peeks through the window.

Some of my medical experiences have helped teach me to be calm, but I also think I was born fairly calm. My dad used to get

---

[10] Thoracostomy tube. These are tubes, often pretty big, inserted between the ribs to remove things from around the lung that are not supposed to be there.

me to clean all the animals we hunted because he was squeamish, and I was not the least bit so. Medical training certainly numbs you up a little bit.

Early in my career, emergency thoracotomies (somewhat dramatically opening up the chest cavity to expose the contents) were more frequently performed in the ED. They have become less common for a number of good reasons. One of the very first ones I performed was a great success, but none of the others have been. I will tell the success story later in a knife wound case—but for now, we're talking about gunshot wounds.

Holes in Hearts

This teen boy went into cardiac arrest immediately prior to arrival per the EMS. His total trip had only been a few minutes. He had a GSW to his left anterior chest, and he was now in cardiac arrest, getting CPR. I had my gown, shield, and gloves ready. I already had on shoe covers. I always wear them in case of tremendously messy, no-warning precipitous deliveries, or these serious and bloody traumas. I also wear them to sneak up on nurses.

"Lots of towels! Everywhere!" That alerted the nurses that a procedure was imminent. They knew what was coming.

As soon as we got him on the bed, I was splashing betadine on his chest. I had already noted the absence of breath sounds on the left, even though EMS was vigorously bagging his ET tube.[11] I asked for towels and blankets because these are usually bloody procedures.

But not this bloody. When I first entered the chest, the blood sprayed everywhere. It was under a lot of pressure. It was a

---

[11] Endotracheal tube. A large tube placed in the trachea for breathing purposes.

tension hemothorax.[12] When I got inside, I soon ceased attempts at saving this kid when I felt the huge hole in the back of his heart, about 3cm across.

In a case that was almost less sad, an actual surgical resident was present soon after the patient's arrival. This was a brief period in my career when these surgeons came to our traumas initially, to be followed by the attending surgeon. Back then, there was sometimes a brief delay waiting for the attending surgeon. This delay was usually not a problem, but every so often . . .

This patient had also been shot in the left chest, but he wasn't quite dead. He was intubated quickly due to his severely decreased responsiveness. He had breath sounds, so my next move was to get better IV access so we could pump blood into him quickly.

I was inserting a large bore central line in his right femoral vein when the surgery resident arrived. Just at that moment, the patient lost his pulse.

"If you don't do it, I will." I used lots of eye contact, trying some leadership technique I'd read about. I knew what he was thinking.

The resident needed a little coaxing to do this procedure. Thoracotomies in the ED have lots of ramifications and can cause career issues that this resident was considering. The indications for the procedure have changed over time, but this patient met all the criteria. I felt strongly this was a good candidate. He had one wound, he had just coded, his brain had been getting oxygen all along, and we had everything else taken care of. We could not make him any worse at this point so, why not?

---

[12] A lot of blood between the lung and chest wall that has been pumped up to a high enough pressure to cause breathing and cardiac dysfunction.

It seemed like a long time, but I am sure it was just seconds before he shared my opinion and opened the chest.

I joined him after securing my central line. I noticed only a moderate amount of blood around the lung. I doubt I could have performed the suturing the surgical resident did to the back of the heart, with the long needle holders and the difficult access. He was able to smoothly repair the small hole that was draining blood from the back of the heart. I was impressed.

I suctioned blood or plugged the hole with my finger or did compressions whenever it did not interfere with his work. The surgical resident tried to put stitches in the hole in front of the heart, but the thin muscle tore. We put a Foley catheter in that hole, inflated it, and pulled it back against the inside wall of the heart. That slowed the bleeding to a trickle. We could see the heart beating effectively now. Soon the patient regained a pulse.

During the few minutes that had transpired in performing the thoracotomy, the nurses had started blood, hooked him to monitors, and inserted the NG tube.[13]

Medical Pearl: Try hard not to tell nurses to do something that they are going to do anyway. Most of them already know exactly what to do in codes or traumas and you will just annoy them or slow them down.

Anyway, the man's pulse persisted. He got a blood pressure consistent with life, but barely. He was no longer bleeding dangerously and seemed to have no other injuries than the holes the resident repaired.

A couple of phone calls later and we were wheeling him upstairs, covering his chest wound with surgical towels and watching him very carefully, expecting something to go wrong. We delivered him to the operating room where he was met by

[13] Nasogastric tube. A small tube inserted in the nose that goes into the stomach (hopefully) to prevent the numerous problems that the organ and its contents can cause.

the attending trauma surgeon, and the chest surgeon. He was alive and with a blood pressure.

Disappointingly and sadly, he did not survive surgery. The chest surgeon told me that the bullet had transected the septum and that he couldn't repair this without a heart bypass machine, which was not available to us.

I also know of a case in our hospital where one of our most prominent trauma surgeons resuscitated a shot-to-death young pregnant woman with a thoracotomy. The nurses said the "scalpel just appeared from nowhere." Maybe all surgeons carry one around.

Otherwise, none of the other emergency thoracotomies have worked in GSWs. Slightly less-invasive procedures frequently save lives. Endotracheal intubations, chest tubes, and large bore lines save lives routinely in the ED, and I've gotten to do my share of these.

A dramatic example of this follows: A young male in his late teens was shot across his chest with a small-caliber gun (a .22). He was unlucky enough to have dropped both his lungs. I was shocked that with lungs that looked so collapsed on x-ray (both of them appearing fist-sized) that he could still be alive and breathing.

Well, barely. I was expecting trouble and was ready to place the chest tube. I started on the right because that pneumothorax[14] was slightly worse. I had placed that tube and I was moving to the other side when the trauma surgeon arrived.

"You're already gowned up, you do it," was the answer to my deferential question about the second tube.

While he was watching, unintentionally making me nervous, I placed the second tube. Things seemed to be going OK, I was just sliding the tube into its final position in his chest

---

[14] Air around, instead of in, the lung. This can cause serious problems.

when the patient arched his back, stiffened and became unresponsive. It looked like he was about to code.

I did not like this, especially since I seemed to cause this turn of events. The patient's "misbehavior" turned into a grand mal seizure, less scary than the alternatives. This ended mercifully quickly, his lungs expanded well, and nothing further bad happened. The seizure seemed to be just a personal jab at me.

GSWs are examples of the real business of EDs. Serious problems that the whole team is prepared for and in some ways prefers to more mundane matters. They are the source of much sorrow, but they are also where smooth trauma care can make a difference. I probably feel my most professional satisfaction when my speed or competence is particularly good on a case and has positive results that might not have occurred with a less-experienced physician, or myself on a different day.

Here is an assortment of memorable cases.

Assorted Cases

Case 1

There was this guy who shot himself in both feet through his cowboy boots. He said he was shooting at rattlesnakes. Hundreds of them. He was a total mystery. What? Why? How?

Case 2

Once this elderly lady was brought in. She had shot herself twice in the left chest with a small caliber pistol. She seemed stable and made it upstairs. I left her room to do something. When I returned a few minutes later, I decided to test for dementia.

"Have you seen me before?" The nurses knew why I asked.

"I wouldn't forget a handsome face like yours," she answered with a weak smile.

Several nurses simultaneously deadpanned cruelly, "Yep, she's got dementia."

Case 3

I saw the police all swarm in, probably twenty officers, when a patient came in dead. They had accidentally shot him, and it was obviously a tragedy that would have broad national repercussions. Fortunately for me, I did not directly care for this politically charged patient.

Case 4

On one shift I saw two fun guys who had been shot, neither of them suffering any serious ill effects. Two weeks later, I saw the same two guys. They had both been reshot. These guys really were fun and also survived these second shots with trivial repercussions (by ED standards). I recognized them, and they seemed happy to see me. I liked these guys.

I do not recall ever seeing them again, but sadly that does not mean much. I wouldn't have recognized them again if they came in shot up until they were unidentifiable, or near dead. One of my buddies might have pronounced them. Maybe they didn't even make it to the hospital? These guys live in a world where being shot is commonplace. It is a sad waste of life.

I've seen people shoot their thighs when drawing their pistols. Someone shot through his camper and took the entire ankle out of his wife. A deer rifle accident partly disemboweled a hunter. I have forgotten dozens of other stories.

Although I am unlikely to forget this one:

The Cheerleader

The victim was a popular teenager in town. A beautiful young girl shot in the mid-chest by her boyfriend. She arrived with nothing much left for us to do. A nurse friend and I went to tell the family. They were crammed into the family room and spilling into the hallway. Twenty to thirty people of all ages.

There is no way to do this well. I made sure my facial expression was somber. Note: under stress, your face doesn't always reflect your inner state well—it is important to self-assess at times. I will also make brief eye contact, then look away if they don't first. (That may break some communication rule, but the grief-shocked are looking for an answer they won't see in my face.)

I tried to make sure I was already sending out nonverbal cues of the worst possible news. I saw them get progressively more horrified as they began to learn that their hope of hopes was being stripped away. Their faces froze, as they stood on the edge of the abyss, awaiting the eons of time squeezed into the seconds it took me to say:

"She did not make it. She has passed a . . ."

A monolithic scream blasted from every soul but mine and the nurse's. It was shockingly loud and solid and steady for several minutes. Like a trained choir with staggered breathing, the individual voices were lost in the unified wail. The stop was abrupt, except for one seven-year-old girl. She kept screaming for three or four seconds until she felt her aloneness, looked around, and fell silent as the family took a breath in preparation for the long haul of grief.

The boy who shot her was flirting with the nurses as the police brought him in for jail clearance. I saw him laughing and saying, "You see what girls make you do?"

I still dread talking to these families. The gunshot victims frequently are young, healthy sons or daughters. Sometimes my job is a little easier because the victim has been living a life of crime and violence for years and the parents have already been grieving their loss for ages. Other times it is as bad as it can possibly be.

4
Men

I am not sure that the "hold my beer" effect has been scientifically verified, but they should not waste the time or money to do a study. It is real. Men and pre-men, young and old, all do risky things that cause themselves and others pain and suffering. Most of the prior GSWs are due to the antics of men, but male human beings are capable of performing an extensive repertoire of mayhem.

For example, a seasoned ED nurse, so seasoned that when she dies, she won't decay for several months—this unflappable nurse gasped when she saw the guy with the chainsaw cut extending from his forehead to his chin. It crossed right over his left orbit, cutting down to the protective bony rim, just missing the eyeball. The wound gaped open and blood covered the rest of his face.

His eyes cracked the seal of blood and both opened as I approached the bed. His left eye really "popped" and was striking in color contrast to its immediate surroundings of bright red. As I was beginning to comment on both the good and the bad aspects of his wound (the lucky eye vs. the unlucky face), he interrupted me with a smile and said, "It's OK, Doc. I'm used to it."

My reply was that if he was used to something like that, he needed a different line of work.

There is a lot of overlap between the sexes regarding unwise behavior, but I doubt that a woman would jump off a three-story building three times sequentially to injure herself enough to get out of the military or was it to get disability? I'm not really sure what *his* plan was. Maybe he hadn't thought it through, either. Regardless, the initial part of his plan worked because he finally broke his ankle. They make these soldiers tough.

Speaking of soldiers, I have not lied to you, nor will I. The following story is difficult to believe. It is possible that some unmentioned shenanigans contributed to these events, although inebriation is unlikely to explain the dogs' behavior.

The injuries included multiple abrasions covering two entire bodies and one badly broken arm out of four. Both patients were remarkably calm regarding what had happened to them. One told me that he had been fighting in Iraq, so this wasn't so bad. I was impressed.

What had happened was: Both men and two dogs were fishing in a small boat. One dog jumped out of the boat perilously close to the lake's large drain. This dog got so close that he began to get sucked in it, as you will have guessed. You might not have guessed that his canine buddy jumped in the water to try to save him, but, in spite of the second dog's assistance, the first dog went down the drain.

As the second dog was also getting sucked in, the dog's human buddy jumped in after *him*. You may not have guessed that the man, also, was getting drained out of the lake due to his miscalculating the hydrodynamics involved. It should surprise no one that the dog's human buddy's human buddy also tried to save him. In other words, everyone that was in the boat was now in the water as the second man tried to save the first man trying to save the second dog trying to save the first dog.

No one was left to save the second man, and none of the rescue attempts were successful. So, in short, a dog then a dog then a man then a man all got sucked into this pipe draining a large lake. It was a long, dark, wet, rough ride with a few turns. All four mammals shot out somewhat safely below the dam. No animals were harmed in the production of this story.

Someone with a dry phone called EMS and to the ED they came. For my tastes, that is one of the scariest episodes I've run across. I don't think I'm claustrophobic, but I would have been horrified flushing along in the dark, just waiting to hit a tight spot, snag, or some grating at the end.

That tale would make a good nightmare.

Something else that would be nightmarish is getting run over by a tank. An unlucky soldier at a machine-gun position got rolled over and crushed into the mud by a tank's track. Other soldiers dug him out, and still others flew him to us. This soldier only sustained a broken humerus and a broken femur. No other injuries. He was redesignated as a lucky soldier. I would have probably added a heart attack to the fractures if I was the crushed party.

Soldiers frequently have bad parachute landings when the big airborne school is in full swing, especially on windy days. Amazingly, I have seen few severe injuries. I have seen several temporarily paralyzed jumpers due to bruising spinal cord injuries that resolved quickly.

I saw a female army captain (I know, I know wrong chapter) with some injuries from this common practice of jumping from airplanes. Soon after departing the plane, a line got wrapped around her neck and began choking her. She fought to remove it, but eventually lost consciousness. She said she regained consciousness briefly before the somewhat hard landing, upon which she broke her leg, a decidedly happy ending considering the other obvious choices. As was mentioned earlier, these soldiers are tough.

In general, even if the men aren't tough, they are so commonly in physically tough positions and so commonly injured that their tragedies seem less tragic. The death or serious injuries of a child or female or especially a female child tend to evoke more powerful emotional responses in us caregivers. If the staff are crying, there's usually a female or child involved. This point will not be proved by the next case.

Father and Son

The middle-aged male arrived in cardiac arrest. He looked like the kind of guy to have a heart attack, centrally obese from eating the same amounts he did in his sportier days. He was probably aware of the potential problem and trying to address it, because on this day, he was out jogging with his son. The father was in town to celebrate the son's graduation from a military school, and they had gone for a morning run together.

The heartwarming scene of a family jog was cut short by the sudden collapse of the older man. The son would have watched as the EMS worked hard on the scene: chest compressions, bagging, shocking, intubating, starting IVs, loading him in the ambulance. The son then found some way to follow behind his dad. When the patient was delivered to us, we continued ACLS[15] treatment for some time, but nothing worked. A massive MI[16] was the most likely cause of the gentleman's death since he was jogging, and plump.

Although you feel sure that these families already *know,* the actual final word from us almost always seems a shock. The distress on the young man's face indicated that he *knew* his father was dead, yet he still somehow looked even more distressed when his worst fears were spoken into reality.

The grief-shocked son rushed by me to the bedside. The son was in his early twenties, tall, well-built, strong, tough—the ideal image of a soldier. After standing beside the warm corpse for a moment, the soldier collapsed across his dad's chest, sobbing. A minute later he arose and, between wails, began praying, almost shouting:

---

[15] Shorthand for, "We mostly followed the treatments taught in the Advanced Cardiac Life Support course."
[16] Myocardial Infarction, or heart attack

"God save him! Revive him from the dead!" I and a dozen nurses, paramedics, techs, and RTs[17] were in attendance.

"I know you have the power, Father. Raise him from the dead!"

There was more of the same for a half hour eternity. The young soldier, having sustained his own grievous wound to the heart, was pleading with and trying to persuade God to heal his dad's dead heart.

The deep sobbing and anguished cries of a young male is a rare and piteous sound. This man induced many familiar voices around me to begin sobbing with him. Many were profoundly shaken by this scene. I was no longer needed, so I returned to other patients.

What was going on here? Why were the nurses so upset?

There was some feeling that this case was somehow a little extra tragic. The nurses and I have seen dozens of middle-age men die suddenly, and we have seen dozens of family members grieve over these deaths.

Some part of it was that many of the nurses had young husbands, a number of them soldiers. The pain of the young man felt close to home for those nurses. But there was more.

I think the situation was similar to us raising our fists at the plane crash site. Then, we were shaking our fists at the helicopter, but there was more. We were also angry at God or the Universe; at who or whatever we believed responsible for this world, where a plane could smash into a mountain and destroy people, leaving the gory evidence of their disassembled lives. Why did this father have to die right at this moment when he and his son were celebrating together?

Why? Why do such horrible things have to happen? Can't someone make this right? Maybe, if those with faith are correct.

---

[17] Respiratory Therapist (or Terrorist?)

Almost everyone eventually pleads for Somebody or Something to do a miracle we know will not happen. That is the heart of the tragedy at hand. With every dead baby, child, mother, father—with each of these sad stories, we have felt the longing in our souls for God, or some vague supernatural machinery, to repair the damage, stop the grief, restore the life. Just this once, at least.

But God or the Universe will not do it. At least not anytime soon. In our ED world, this longing is not fulfilled. There are some miraculous or unexpected surprises, and some near-misses, but where it really counts, when death really can only be defeated by the Creator, when we really ask from the depth of our souls—we will be told no.

In the ED, after rubbing shoulders with hundreds of the dead and dying and their grieving families, we have learned not to ask the question. In the early years, we may ask a hundred times, but at some point, we finally learn that the disease will not relent, the injury will not heal, the death will be final.

The young man's cries of "Raise him!" reminded us of longings we had put away. He pulled us back into our younger minds, a place of searching, questioning, wondering—in a time when the years ahead made us feel the need to understand.

The young need to plan and hope, hence the need for understanding. At some point as we grow old, predicting the future loses its urgency. The questions change.

"What if?" becomes "What is?" We focus on: what is our realm now, what can we do, what can we really expect? We identify and cherish what we love, and cherish them even more because we know, we can *feel*, that none of us will last forever.

Those with faith, of course, are trying to play a longer game. Faith is not powerless, by any means, to diminish suffering and aid with healing. The faithful even have hopes that everything will be made right. But most of that is for the next world, not this one. Those of us in the ED are stuck here, now, in the only world we have, where the bigger the question, the less likely you are to get an answer.

It lessens the pain, it helps you move on, it helps people who need you here and now—when you work and think at your pay grade, do your job, plant your feet. Don't let the hard questions you can't answer befuddle your brain so much that you can't answer the easy questions.

No one has it all figured out. Lots of people have tried for millenia, with libraries written on theodicy, theologies of suffering, philosophies of suffering. All the big answers also raise big questions.

Everyone, from the most gullible supernaturalist to the most skeptical materialist, believes something very weird at some point in their paradigm. We all live in glass houses, and none of us should cast stones.

Do not spend too long lingering at the bedside of pleading sons. Call the chaplain—it's their job.

Women are making great gains in the professions, but I do not think it likely that women will ever be the equal of men when it comes to breaking the law. The vast majority of prisoners are men, and I will predict, here in writing, that this will not change much as women increase in numbers elsewhere.

So, I have included my prisoner accounts here, under "Men." Interestingly, these guys are generally well-behaved in our setting. The polite murderer may even say, "I'm having a bad day," when he shows up to the ED for jail clearance after walking up behind a bicyclist and shooting him in the back of the head (again, true story).

These well-behaved guys are still not always easy to deal with. It is frequently hard to tell real complaints from "Incarceritis," a made-up problem in attempts to avoid or delay imprisonment. They also are very frequently afraid of needles and don't hold still when you pull out the Taser darts.

They typically respond well to being treated with respect, but if I am particularly chummy with a prisoner, I will also be careful to thank the officer who caught him.

I try to orchestrate this as a simultaneous, peaceful three-way conversation. As long as the prisoner feels he is not despised, he is often willing to accept his and his captor's role with dignity. This is not always the case, of course.

This young man was lying back on a hospital bed, chained to a railing. "Jail clearance, AIDS," was on the note. This was back when AIDS was a death sentence for every patient and the world didn't quite have a feel for how easily or not it spread around. This man was all bloody and angry, having recently fought some fellow civilian or his captors. He had not accepted defeat. I was troubled by the combination of the visible blood and the invisible AIDS.

His female captor was small but intimidating—stiff and bulging with body armor, with an assortment of weapons swinging about her waist. She approached close to the foot of the bed as I stood nearby, calculating risks.

The prisoner spat in defiance at her, a bloody spray. I stepped back, but the policewoman sprang from the foot of the bed and plunged her knee into his chest, pinning him firmly to the headboard. I remember the fear in his eyes and the message of, "OK, you win."

The police officer was responding to a lethal threat, and her jump was faster, and her knee was much more effective than I would have predicted. I was impressed. The patient was treated and then taken away to jail.

Another young prisoner used a different approach. He apparently was also not interested in jail and had not reached the peace that comes with "you win":

The two police walked the patient by our station and placed him in the room. There was no window in the door that the patient audibly locked a few minutes later, trapping himself alone in the room. The police yelled for the key and the nurses scrambled to find it.

We could hear a huge commotion from within the room for the several minutes it took to find the universal key and open the door. I was watching the door closely, wondering what work there would be for me. When the officers burst into the room, they found nothing.

Nothing. Well, a destroyed room, broken sink and some demolished ceiling tiles, but no prisoner.

"The door!" someone yelled, and the police ran in pursuit.

The man was not captured anytime soon. As he was brought in, he had somehow noticed the building layout. Maybe he helped build it? Once in the room, he climbed up on the sink, then into the ceiling. He then was able to crawl over the wall separating his room from the ambulance entrance. From there he made his final dash from the hospital. We were all impressed.

It is hard work staying free or making a living when the law is not on your side. I am not sure that this next case involved any illegalities other than the initial stabbing, but I heard rumors afterwards that the patient was a drug dealer.

Emergency Thoracotomy

It was late some night, probably a weekend. We were alerted by lots of noise and we swarmed and surrounded the EMS as they entered with the stretcher and patient. Nurses, EMS, an

RT, med techs, x-ray techs and myself. We rolled him into the trauma room as chest compressions were being performed, EMS pumping deeply on the patient, who was supine on the rolling stretcher.

"Stab wound to chest, he coded en route!"

I looked around the trauma room and checked out my options. The resident was ready and was capable. Two big IVs were going.

"Can you intubate him?" I asked the resident, Dr E—.

"I got it." The RT helped him with the airway.

"Thoracotomy[18] tray!" I had made my decision. The patient had penetrating chest trauma and lost his pulse minutes ago. I couldn't make him any worse.

Someone handed me some betadine, and I started splashing it on his chest. There was a tiny cut on the front left chest where the knife had entered.

Dr. E— had him intubated by the time I had opened up the tray. I'm sure my heart was pounding, but I didn't notice. I was ready.

"Hold compressions!"

The scalpel felt a little awkward as I sliced through his skin from sternum to as far back as I could get. In the ED, we rarely use scalpels that way. I cut following the curve of his ribs in a line beneath his chest muscles. I then used scissors to cut through fat and muscle. I was working fast because I knew I had to, not because I was practiced.

I reached the pleura and made a cut, then extended it. His lung began ballooning into view each time he was bagged.

I got the rib spreader (this was only the second, or maybe third time I'd picked one up), figured out how to assemble it, and popped it into position. I then turned the crank, ripping my

---

[18] "Otomy" means cut, "Ostomy" means puncture, so thoracotomy vs thoracostomy. Confusion may occur at numerous points.

opening wide to allow access to the heart. I also used the side hammer chisel in the tray to increase the width of the opening all the way to the sternum.

At this point, just opening him up would have fixed any tension pneumothorax or hemothorax that might have been killing him. There was not enough blood around the lung to have been exsanguinating him. The answer was deeper in.

"Pull the lung out of the way. Use this thing." A nurse had gloved up and was ready and took the retractor from me.

I could now see the purplish heart that was not beating. I could see the little stab wound towards the front of the heart. I slid my hand in, hoping to pump some blood to his brain by squeezing the heart forward against his chest wall.

Within a squeeze or two, I noticed some big blood clots bulging from the stab wound in the pericardium. I squeezed some more and pushed a handful of clot out. I was about to make the cut bigger when the heart began beating in my fingers.

The heartbeat quickly became a vigorous, rhythmic movement. That was good. It had to be more effective than my CPR. As I watched this spectacle, I reassessed.

The patient was lying with a huge bloody gash opening his chest. His heart was visibly beating, and his lung was visibly inflating. He had a real pulse.

Now I was getting scared, or maybe feeling what was already there. Before, he was dead. I couldn't really make him worse; I didn't have anything to lose. Now, I could make things worse, so I had a lot to lose (even more so for the patient).

He already had lots of IV access and was getting blood; he was on the monitor.

"Blood pressure."

As the cuff inflated, I looked for bleeding in his chest and watched his pumping heart. I don't recall the first pressure, but it was good news.

Now what?

I laid some sterile towels over his chest, and I stripped off my bloody gloves and gown and headed to the door.

"I need the trauma surgeon and chest surgeon!"

I kept an eye on things from a distance as RTs put him on the vent and nurses hovered over every detail. He wasn't requiring much extra care at this point. No pressors, no sedation.

The chest surgeon called back first, and I gave him my spiel.

"OK," he said.

I was left to ponder precisely what that meant. The trauma surgeon called soon after. I gave him the story, mentioning that the chest surgeon was aware.

"Which one of us do you want? Me or thoracic?" Dr. J— asked.

"Both! I need both of you," I urged excitedly, without a moment's delay. The trauma surgeon mercifully came quickly and took the man upstairs. I presume the chest surgeon met him in the OR, but I was told the man had not required any extensive surgery.

I was also told about a week later that the man continued to do well and left the hospital against advice.

Foreign Bodies

I think that's all for the wrong-side-of-the-law patients. Of course, even when no laws are being broken, men's work or play often presents opportunities for injury.

In this "work" category, I saw a sturdy young farmer who was injured as well as being held against his will in the back of the ambulance. He was being held by a pitchfork that had penetrated his medial leather boot, then his medial sock, then his ankle. Palindromically[19], the pitchfork's long, curved tine then exited his lateral ankle, lateral sock, and lateral boot. This pitchfork had a sturdy, all-metal handle. EMS would have sawn off a wooden handle, but they had nothing onboard their truck to deal with this thick metal pipe welded to the fork with its three tines.

EMS had managed to maneuver the man into the back of the ambulance, with the pitchfork spanning cross-wise. I am sure that was painful and difficult. However, it was unfortunate that in this configuration, the angles of leg, pitchfork, and vehicle conspired to jamb the end of the handle into a corner of the ambulance's cabinetry.

The man was being held by the handle of the pitchfork which had now wedged itself tightly. His pain of "nine" (my estimate) was activated with any movement of himself, his stretcher, the pitchfork, or his foot. He was pinned in place, and any attempts to release him were met with loud screaming.

In addition to the piteous cries, I was bothered by the thought of all the further harm movement would cause the bones and ligaments and cartilage of his ankle and imagined all the crunching that was causing the pain.

A careful engineering study, an ambulance bay conference, and a quick jiggling of all the components present did not indicate any easy way of removing this patient or the pitchfork. I was surrounded by capable, mechanically-minded people who shared my lack of a good plan.

Not having a good plan does not prevent planning, and so I proceeded to sell the charge nurse on the best idea I could come up with. The nurses would have to break several rules, but I was able to convince them that this was the best option. Once the nurses were in, they were all in and made things happen.

---

[19] I and Microsoft Word thought that I made up that adjective. Dr. Google says it is a real word.

We got a powerful sedative, propofol, and planned to zonk him fairly heavily in the back of the ambulance. He was on a monitor with airway equipment about. It was reasonably safe. There was plenty of help, but the room was a little tight.

We splashed some betadine on the protruding end of the spike. The merciful helper entered through the front and produced the milky drug for his IV. I stood ready at the double door, my mercy setting on "mute." I was gearing myself up for a fight.

I visually verified that the farmer was out, mouth agape and slumped back against his gurney, the silence of no-screaming softly falling in white flakes around us. *Medical Pearl: Propofol is a wonderful drug and has dramatically diminished the level of suffering in EDs.*

As an experienced hand at objects being not-where-they-should-be, I knew that considerable force would be necessary to remove this one, and that care should be taken in the direction of travel of this force as I applied it.

I braced my foot against the side of the ambulance and firmly pulled the cold metal handle in what I surmised was the opposite of the path it took on the way in. I had to put a lot of my weight into it. That did not surprise me.

Out it came! And so did he. It was a quiet gurney ride into the ED, where he awakened without issues. Propofol commonly causes amnesia in patients regarding the time around the procedure. Giving propofol in this case may have even given me amnesia because I recall nothing else about the case.

It is likely he didn't have much damage. Musculoskeletal structures are pretty tough and seem to know how to dodge penetrating objects.

I saw a guy once who had shot a nail through three fingers, pinning them together, side by side like some kind of Boy Scout salute. Although the nail appeared to cross through the middle of the fingers, it had in fact missed all the bones. After the nail's removal, his fingers worked normally. *Medical Pearl: These nails are harder to pull out than you expect and often have little tabs that grab the skin.*

Of course, a later infection would be a disaster, but with lots of antibiotics nowadays, a disaster is much less likely than it was just a few years ago.

Here's another penetrating story. It has been long enough that I should remind you that I am not going to lie. All of these stories are true. This particular story is not incredible, but it shows that people have a hard time believing you at times.

The young male landscaper was sweaty, but not just from working. He was sitting on the end of the bed, in shorts with his legs hanging off, the left one impaled by a coat-hanger wire. A weed-eater machine had thrown the wire, and it completely penetrated his calf, with about six inches protruding on either side, just above sock level.

"You gotta put me to sleep, Doc!"

"What? No, this will be nothing; you probably won't even feel it as I pull it out. It will be no big deal. I can't risk putting you to sleep for this," I said.

Since you have read this far in the book, you will know that my words were of no effect. Neither were his. He continued to beg to be put to sleep in repeated pleadings as I continued to plead my case. All the words were falling on deaf ears, four of them total.

Our conversation continued as I was squatted down in front of him, cleaning the leg and its metal accessory with betadine. I mostly looked up and talked to the man as I slowly began pulling the wire, cautious to precisely reverse its recent trajectory.

"You gotta put me to sleep, you gotta . . ." he was near tears.

Shock silenced him when his eyes focused on the wire I held up between both our faces.

"I told you it wouldn't hurt."

He still didn't quite believe me until he had inspected the empty puncture wounds for himself.

The level of pain produced by an injury, procedure, nurse, or yours truly is hard to predict, especially for those without medical experience. Once you are under the skin, a lot of things don't hurt much. Even lethal injuries don't always hurt much. Being stabbed to death is frequently painless, with the unstoppable bleeding occurring in some inaccessible place, unable to be stopped until it is too late. It's often a matter of drifting off to sleep. Even the initial stab is often passed off as, "I thought he had just punched me."

However, problems with kidneys, peritoneal linings[20], and bones are rarely painless. The orthopedic injuries can be the worst. "Ortho's here," I used to darkly comment as I entered the department, alerted to the orthopedists by the presence of screaming. This was before the routine use of effective sedating medications or even before the invention of the best of these drugs.

In the old days, I was at the bedside when a local orthopedist was treating an elbow dislocation. He was holding the patient's arm. The doctor had one hand behind the patient's elbow and his other hand on the man's forearm. He was just casually talking to the patient, "No it's really not a big . . ." when he stopped midsentence and suddenly pulled with one hand and pushed with the other, manipulating the arm. The patient prepared to scream in agony but discovered that he didn't need to. His elbow was back in place.

Nowadays, I look forward to dislocations because you typically get dramatic improvement in symptoms with minimal suffering due to the new drugs. Shoulder dislocations are always a welcome sight.

Patellar dislocations are also rewarding to treat. These typically are painful, frightening-looking "knee dislocations."

---

[20] These are the thin linings that cover most inner surfaces and are responsible for the pain of numerous conditions, appendicitis being perhaps the most famous.

Real knee dislocations are a very big, leg-losing-potential kind of deal. Knee-cap dislocations are a whole different ballgame and rarely cause serious problems.

One patellar dislocation belonged to a high school soccer player, stuck in the ambulance entrance on her gurney. She was a young teen in a cheery uniform surrounded by quiet or moaning, apparently very ill individuals. She was nervously scanning her surroundings, sitting with the head of her EMS gurney slightly raised.

"That's the kneecap that's out, the whole knee is not out." She tensed as I pointed to the patella itself, afraid I was going to touch the bizarrely malformed knee, with the patella shoved laterally, stretching her skin tight.

"It's no big deal." I felt the weight of the impending death potential around me, those lying forlorn in the purgatory of the ambulance bay, not outside, but not exactly in the hospital. I needed to get to those patients. The department was full, and it could be hours before a bed opened up. The nurses were all at their capacity. I made my pitch.

"It will only hurt for a second if we just pop it in. You could do it yourself. It will be way less pain all total if we just do it now, instead of waiting until we get some more meds." I spent a considerable amount of precious time on this gamble. I did not lose when, finally, the patient and the mother were in agreement. This would now save us all a lot of time.

We were all ready. I straightened her leg swiftly and pushed the patella back into position. The girl opened her mouth to scream, but the pain was already gone, and the knee now looked normal, and she was fine. The mother huffed, "Well if I'd had known it was that easy, I would have done it myself." You cannot win. You will read those same words in a little story in the chapter "Children."

For now, I'd like to contrast the above story with the following one. Imagine the exact same situation above (I do not recall the sport this second girl played). The accounts diverge just at the point of relocation. When the girl in the current story opened her mouth to scream, she did just that, for longer than I thought possible. After a brief breath, she resumed the blood-curdling scream until the entire ambulance bay was dreading the horrors to come at my hands.

Wait a minute. How did we get talking about all these girls in the men's section? My apologies. I will get us back on track.

This next story could only happen to a man, for three reasons:

"I fell off the ladder." (Reason one: Ladder injuries are 76% male.)

"This made my groin hernia pop out ..." (Reason two: Inguinal hernias are 90% male.)

"And I scratched my penis." (Reason three: No comment.)

The history was straightforward. My exam indicated that the hernia was firm and not reducible. This would indicate an incarcerated hernia. This was a problem that had to go away fairly soon, or it would become a real problem, with the result of a section of dead bowel.

I tried coaxing the mass back in his groin repeatedly, with no success. It was too tender for me to be vigorous with him; the tenderness added to my concern because it may have meant the blood supply was being compromised.

It was time for drugs. I sedated him fairly heavily to make reduction of the painful hernia possible. I tried to maneuver the mass back into place. He was sedate enough that I was able to try as hard as I thought was safe, but there was nothing more I could do. This was no longer my territory.

It was time for a surgeon.

"Dr. B—, I have this guy who fell off a ladder. He says it made his hernia pop out further and now it is irreducible."

He came right in. The patient was back with us, wide awake after his sedation.

After a brief exam, the surgeon was not convinced. "This may be a lymph node."

The surgeon asked the patient, "Sir, do you have any sores?"

The patient said yes by immediately pulling down his trousers to reveal the "scratch." It was clearly an infectious lesion, an STD[21] that was also clearly causing the swollen lymph node.

This surgeon normally has a little edge and is not above sarcasm. However, he would not kick a man when he was down. He flashed a grin at me and ambled off, leaving me with the nonsurgical patient with the non-surgical complaint. We were back in my territory.

I was very happy I did not somehow reduce the lymph node. So, the ladder fall was mostly irrelevant, and we gave him an injection and a prescription and released him back to the broader world.

Assorted Cases

Case 1

I once had a guy with both a heart attack and a stroke simultaneously. This combination is not that awfully rare in the very infirm, but this guy was youngish and both conditions were sudden and dramatic.

His MI was obvious on the EKG[22] and "Code STEMI"[23] was called. His stroke was obvious due to his profound unilateral weakness, and "Code S" was called. Both conditions were unequivocal and serious and time-sensitive.

---

[21] You will have to look this up yourself.

[22] ElectroKardioGram. Or ElectroCardioGram. What is an EEG? Electroencephalogram. What is an EGG? An egg. Hahahaha!

[23] ST-Elevation Myocardial Infarction. I recommend consulting Dr. Google.

Both of these protocols entail major interventions with life-threatening consequences, multiple specialists, and reams of supporting personnel, as well as a cruelly ticking clock.

I recall that everyone was frightened by everyone else's problem. The IR team, blithe about sticking a tube into the blood vessels in his brain and pulling a clot out, were nervous about the appearance of his EKG and called me over to look at his monitor, which, yes, indicated he was having an MI. We already knew that.

The cardiologist was worried about catheterizing someone who had just had someone fiddling in their brain. I had to do a little reassuring.

From my perspective, it was easy. The stroke had to be treated, almost regardless of risk, because the disability was so horrible. The stroke-busting blood thinners would help with treating his heart.

The MI had to be treated, almost regardless of the risk, because it could easily kill him. It wouldn't help to treat his stroke if he was dead.

Case 2

"Why did you call the police on me?" The man glared across the table.[24]

"Well, the phone number in the chart didn't work and you have a problem that is an emergency," I replied.

"What?" he asked, obviously annoyed. He had just been here the day before and gotten a chest x-ray. Another doctor (not me! Yay!) missed a pretty large pneumothorax, 30% was the radiologist's estimate. This was life-threatening.

---

[24] We occasionally ask the police to run down patients when life-threatening issues are at hand. In urgent situations, the police will find and notify patients to call us or direct an ambulance to return the patient to us if there are problems (usually the patient has given us bad phone numbers).

He sat there in his trench coat, sizing me up. Definitely trying and succeeding in intimidating me.

"Are you having any trouble breathing? Any chest pain?" He said no to both, but he did say he was having trouble sleeping when he lay down.

Case 3

I saw a man who had been laying on his belly for six months. He had grown so obese that he couldn't walk or even roll over now. I asked his family, "Do you bring him what he needs to eat, or anything he asks for?"

"Anything he asks for," was the answer given. The man died when he was rolled over upstairs.

Case 4

I did not treat this patient, but I am 90% sure I saw him wheeling down the hall. I may have confused him with the other few patients I've seen with similar presentations.

This patient was sitting upright on the gurney that was being hurriedly pushed into the trauma room. He was flanked by police and EMS. He looked excited and maybe a little overly so. His excitement was probably due to the large kitchen knife handle rising proud from his anterior chest.

"Don't take it out, it's evidence! Dust it for fingerprints!" The patient with the knife commanded us.

Case 5

I saw a farmer who got his leg hung up in a tractor-mounted hole digger. It ripped everything off of his lower leg except a bare, dry tibia sprinkled with dirt.

Case 6

This patient was a police combat instructor. He was sixty years old and said he could do ten pushups on just one thumb. I do not know how the topic came up. I watched him do ten pushups on just one thumb. His thumb was twice as thick as mine. I was impressed.

Case 7 & 8

I have seen two patients with a blown pupil and no other problems. I am not counting the glass eye from medical school. Both these patients had completely normal exams and no symptoms beyond a little blurriness in the eye with the large pupil.

The diagnosis was successful in the first patient because he had dropped a clue: "I was fishing in Florida."

A connection suggested itself and I asked, "Did you use one of those scopolamine patches for nausea?"

The answer was yes. Some of the potent chemical had gotten on his finger and then into his eye.

In the second case, the sequence was backwards. An ophthalmologist stopped by my cubicle. He announced he had been summoned for a confusing blown pupil. I mentioned the patch and fishing story, and another mystery was solved when this second patient admitted to both.

It is a fun and rare treat to show up a specialist. Do not rejoice in such a thing, because you will soon be brought low. You do not want any specialists looking for payback.

Case 9

Speaking of ophthalmologists: I saw a man who had wrecked into the back of a logging trucking. His injury was a two-finger thick, foot-long "splinter" of wood that penetrated his eyeball and lodged in the back of the socket. It did not reach his brain, according to the CT (although MRI is better for wood).

I described all this to the eye doctor on call, who upon seeing the case for himself exclaimed, "You weren't lying!"

5

Women

Everyone likes delivery stories; no one likes miscarriage stories. Here's several of both. To set the appropriate tone for you, I will randomly intersperse happy stories with horrible stories, because that's what dealing with the medical side of pregnancy is like.

You have to keep both sides, happy vs. horrible, in your head. Very commonly, as I discharge a patient, particularly with a diagnosis of threatened miscarriage, I will try to counter whichever side I think the patient is fixating on too strongly.

"So, you're saying everything is fine?" says the too-cheery, five-weeks pregnant woman with vaginal bleeding.

"No, I'm saying your bleeding could very well be the start of a miscarriage. You and your ultrasound look fine, but the bleeding . . ."

Now she changes sides and looks too sad. I apply verbal counterpressure in the opposite direction.

"But I have seen lots of bleeding like yours in girls who had normal babies." Of course, now she is too cheerful, so . . .

We lob the tennis ball of emotions between these two perspectives. In reality, it may be impossible for any normal person to simultaneously feel strongly and also be noncommittal. Since I'm not the pregnant party, I don't feel so strongly; so, I can calmly see both sides. I don't expect the patient to be objective, but I feel it's important to attempt to prepare them for whichever way things go.

Into the Breech

"Dr. McAnonymous, we need you in Seventeen!"

That's how this works. It is always an interruption; it never just flows like the tale in a good book does.

"Seventeen!" The voices are trying to make sure I dropped everything else. "Right now!"

I did drop everything and scurried down the hall.

In Room 17, I saw a rotund teenager in distress on the bed. Her age was also seventeen, "abdominal pain" was on the chart, and this was immediately confirmed with a glance at the patient. She was holding her belly and grimacing with pain. She was "Not pregnant!"

The nurse's eyes told me to look further south.

Her mom was standing at the head of the bed near the door. The room was a little tight. I gathered the above information as I squeezed across the room to get to her abdomen. I found the problem a little further away from the head of the bed. I saw two small blue legs sticking out between the large legs of the girl who was *not* not pregnant.

"Gloves!" My shoe covers were already on. It was too late for a gown, so I buttoned my lab coat.

I pressed a finger into one leg, *hmm capillary refill is good.* I don't know what that really means in a breech delivery, but at the time I thought it meant the baby was still viable, and that I would need to hurry.

I began gently pulling on the legs as the mom pushed. There seemed to be lots of movement in the right direction, a pelvis, then a torso was just easing out; things were looking up, *This is working fine* ... until the head got stuck.

Uh-oh. That's when I thought, Maybe I should have held junior inside and wheeled them both upstairs.

Anyway, I had read about several procedures for breech deliveries, and after a little bit of pulling and pushing (mostly random) from me and the mom, the baby's head popped out.

The baby's entire face and head were white. This extreme pallor was made even more striking due to the deep blue of the rest of the baby. In spite of this unfavorable coloring, the baby breathed, and so did I.

I passed the blue and white baby off to the peds team—I was ecstatic to see that someone had called them. They took that scary responsibility away from me, and I was grateful. I turned back to the new mom and grandmom.

"We now know the cause of your abdominal pain." This was followed by a long discussion filled with warnings about the blue and white baby. Pointing out the dire possibilities ended up being unnecessary, because the baby pinked up quickly and ended up being fine.

I know there are some who doubt that it is possible, but I believed that this girl did not know she was pregnant. She gave me no hint that she had been hiding a secret, and she did have the appropriate figure to hide a pregnancy.

I have heard of other occult pregnancies. It is not always so easy to know what's going on with women. There are a lot of moving parts, and frequently there are two females in the same body. Assume all women are pregnant.

This other woman was sent to me from the ED. I was a resident rotating in Labor and Delivery, and this lady was transferred to us "intoxicated" plus "in labor." Other than the alcohol, things appeared straightforward.

She had a protuberant belly, and every few minutes she would grimace and try to push out what was causing her pain. We had great trouble keeping her in bed or getting her to cooperate with anything.

After the usual wrestling match that occurs with drunk patients, we were able to get an ultrasound probe on her. I searched around for the baby, but all I saw was nothing. Nothing but black, no baby.

After some intense reflection, I decided that it was just a huge bladder. This lady was suffering from urinary retention.

We quickly cured her pains with a catheter and delivered a lot of healthy urine.

I delivered a baby in a Volvo with cloth seats (I wondered about resale issues), one in the lobby bathroom, several in ED beds, one in the elevator, a couple in cars with vinyl seats.

I do not recall the type of seat in this one car. But I sure remember the baby. This was the case where I delivered an en caul baby. The mother was seated on the front passenger side. The baby was floating peacefully in a huge bag of fluid, sitting in the bewildered mother's lap.

The hard work had already been done by the mom. It was an en route en caul. It was night in the ambulance entrance, a little dimly lit for deliveries. The nurses were getting supplies, I was donning gloves, my shoe covers were in place, and we jumped in headfirst.

The mom was quiet at this point; the big bag had been pushed out. Typically torn, somehow this sac had remained intact and the baby was suspended in what looked like a clear beach ball. The newborn occasionally kicked its extremities.

I prepared to cut open the amniotic sac, appropriately nervous that I could also injure the baby in the darkness if not careful. I was also more nervous about the overall course of action. I had never heard any details of delivering these babies, I was only aware that it could happen.

I had the feeling that I could easily make things worse. The baby looked like he didn't want to be disturbed. He looked fine; so did mom. How long could this last? Surely not long, so I made my cut. The fluid ran out the small opening, then gushed out as I deflated the whole sac by tearing.

After that, it was a normal ED precipitous delivery. The nurses handed me clamps and scissors and towels, and we got them both inside and shipped them upstairs.

In case this sounds fun, you are too cheery, so it is time for a sad story. Miscarriages are an odd thing. They involve deep questions of what is alive, what is human. The effects these extremely common events have on patients and the rest of us profoundly varies from case to case. To illustrate, I will mention a few odd examples.

I saw an unusual case where the patient brought in what she thought was a fetus. She was not particularly disturbed. Now, it is not unusual for patients to bring in what has come out of them, nor is it unusual for them to not be particularly disturbed by the occurrence. In this case, what was unusual was that she brought the hapless fetus to us, pressed in a book. She opened a book and handed me a sandwich bag containing a perfectly flat, three-centimeter diameter disk of off-white flesh with two black spots near its midline.

In contrast, this other lady wanted a funeral for her fetus. Actually, I don't think the mom wanted the funeral, just the grandmom. I'll have to start back at the beginning with this case.

The nurses and EMS slid the nineteen-year-old girl and the sheet she was lying on over onto the bed in T6. She was calm and collected and had a bloody, obviously dead fetus and some surrounding debris between her legs. It was maybe an eighteen-week gestation. She was mature, handling her own emotions, and I was able to make decisions regarding her wishes. She was interested in the idea of having the remains taken care of by us and indicated that she was interested in leaving all of this behind her as quickly as possible—no naming, no rituals, just move on.

We cleaned her up, examined her (no problems), and I got ready to send her upstairs. The situation seemed so neatly tied up that someone questioned whether we even had to send her to L&D now, since she'd completed delivering the fetus and placenta. I was not entirely comfortable that the placenta was intact (I was also sending it and the fetus to pathology), so I pushed back with:

"We should send her up. Maybe there are some retained fragments, or there could even be a twin."

Later that shift, I was surprised and annoyed to hear that L&D had lambasted our staff for not cleaning her up before bringing her upstairs. I knew this was unjust because I had even helped with this; we had cleaned her like we normally do.

The next evening I was approached by an administrative nurse and heard the "more-to-the-story." It seems that the patient's mother had pushed the idea of a memorial service for the fetus, which now had a name. I knew this was not the patient's original wishes, but it is OK to change your mind.

This was fine by all of us, but when the time came for the hospital to release the remains, two individual fetuses were found—the one I had sent to pathology and another one sent to the morgue.

The ED did not send any remains to the morgue. Now the L&D complaint about our lack of cleaning made sense. The second fetus delivered on the way upstairs, creating a new bloody mess that we were falsely accused of ignoring.

Why was I now involved again? The administrator was asking me to call the family to explain the fact that there were actually two fetuses and to ask for instructions from the mom regarding the memorial. The L&D residents had swapped out by now, so I was the only doctor around that had actually participated in the patient's care. Great.

I called the teenager first. She gave me permission to talk with her mother and added, "Do whatever Mom wants." That difficult telephone discussion went much better than I expected.

Of course, treating women patients is not all about pregnancy. Even after the age of pregnancy risk passes, these women are just as much trouble as men and sometimes trickier to diagnose. An example is their weird MI presentations. The biggest problems in the younger women are still usually pregnancy related, unless you take some precautions:

I re-entered the room of the young bride. She was twenty-one and had some minor gyn complaint. Her husband, two years younger, was now by her side.

"Can we talk in front of him?" I asked.

"Of course, he's my husband," she said as she held his arm and gazed at him.

I started, "Well, since you've had a tubal ligation—"

She stopped me.

"Just a second," she said to me.

She turned her face back to her husband and said, "Honey, there's something I need to tell you. We can't ever have children."

She then indicated that I could continue my discussion. The husband seemed to be stunned into deep thought. Perhaps for the first time.

I treated another interesting case that involved a delivery but no baby.

The Case of the Rubber Ducky

This seventeen-year-old looked poised and comfortable sitting in the gyn room. Her counselor from the home for troubled girls sat nearby. Brief greetings and a few questions, then, "I've got a rubber ducky stuck inside," with a glance downward.

First, I retrieved a chaperone. Then we retrieved sponge forceps, lights, and a speculum. We got "mom" into position in the stirrups. She was self-possessed and good-natured and handling the whole situation in a manner that helped things go well. She could have made the process a lot harder, and a lot of patients would have.

And it was a process. The rubber ducky was held in place by a combination of lack of adequate space as well as a vacuum effect. This would take some effort.

The little orange cap glowed in the light. "It's vertex!" I said cheerily. This really was good news, because if the head had not been oriented outwards, the featureless bottom of the duck would have presented nothing to grab. I don't know if the girl knew what vertex meant exactly, but the nurse did. Keeping the nurse from getting too serious would help the patient stay calm, and I needed to keep the patient's anxiety level low.

Cooperation on her part was necessary to prevent this delivery from escalating to a more-risky sedated procedure[25]. I grasped the head and cap with the sponge forceps. It took a significant amount of twisting and pulling to deliver the ducky, as well as pushing on the patient's part. "Push!" Out it popped.

"It's a boy! No, it's a girl. Uhm, I don't know!"

The patient was suitably happy after the delivery but showed no cross-species maternal instincts.

I hope the future went well for that girl. She had the makings of a nurse or doctor or anything she wanted to be. Her life would not have been easy so far, or she would not have been in the group home. A tough family, drugs, crime, or abuse—something was up. Most likely she was under attack from a combination of those scourges.

If she was going to make it in the world, achieve some stable happiness, she would have to sail through some headwinds. Bon voyage and Godspeed to her and all those girls in the boat with her.

I guess the rubber ducky story is a happy one, but there is always some sharp edge to ED tales. It reminds me of the times

---

[25] This event occurred before great sedatives were available. Lots of Demerol was used for shoulder reductions and the like. When we entered the ED and heard screams, it meant "Ortho is here." The good old days were not.

that a child will run after me as I leave a room, wanting to play some more, starved for fun or attention. It's sad when the ED is more fun for a child than home. Children and teens often have hard lives that press in around them, trying to extinguish their spark.

You can't let the problems of patients pull you in too deep, because soon your friends and family will need your help, or you may need extra strength to help yourself in some new disaster. You have to put the oxygen on yourself first if you want to help others. It still is tempting to give your hearts to all these needy souls, but there are good reasons not to.

Of most importance as a practitioner, you have to keep enough distance between you and the patient so you can think clearly. You cannot save a child who needs intubation if your eyes are full of tears. The crying is Mom's job.

Another reason to not give your heart to patients too quickly is that medicine is not a world of normal relationships. As a practitioner, you are a professional. You may be a friend to your patients, but when the conditions are right, they will turn on you and sue the pants off of you. For your own sanity, you must accept this.

I learned of this aspect of the doctor/patient relationship early on. Learning this early has made me more objective, more careful, less judging of other clinicians, more able to say no, and more able to reserve my deepest affections for my family. Patients, administrators, or coworkers, shouldn't be allowed to damage your family (I do not deny some families are more trouble than they are worth—no judgement from me if you pick the hospital instead).

Anyway, back to the cases. This one involves my first lawsuit.

Lawsuit

Vaginal deliveries after c-section had just become the "right thing to do" when I was a resident. This was a way to reduce the too-common c-section. Prior to those years, c-sections were routinely repeated to avoid uterine tears. The post-c-section vaginal delivery approach fell back out of favor a few years later, and I have some insight regarding why.

I was a second-year resident, covering the entire hospital—deliveries, newborns, adults, all admissions. There were two first-year interns, also. One of them phoned me.

"I've got this lady in labor. Her last delivery was a c-section. I've already called the attending. We're going to let her deliver vaginally." Those might not be the precise words he used, but it was made precisely clear to me that I was not needed.

I had been made superfluous by the attending's involvement. This was not unusual at all in those days and at that community hospital. The attendings were very involved in patient care without expecting the entire hierarchical structure that ruled in more academic settings.

I did not hear about this at the time, but during the labor the next morning the lady's uterus did rupture, an emergency C-section was necessary, and the baby was born with a badly damaged brain.

The first indication of any problem for me was when I was approached by my residency attendings later that next day. Noticing the legal risk, they instructed me to place a note on the chart verifying that the first-year had called the OB attending. I wrote something very like: "Dr X informed me that he had seen this patient and had already discussed her case with Dr Y."

Within a year, the intern, the attending, and I were all sued.

"If you treat people well, they won't sue you," said one of our favorite OB attendings. He was sued within a year of saying this.

I had to go to two meetings that lasted fifteen minutes each. I had no input regarding any trial or settlement. The case was settled out of court by the lawyers. My share was deemed to be a hundred and twenty-five thousand dollars, just enough to get me listed in the National Practitioner Databank.

What I learned from this experience was that the only people who pay for all these lawsuits are patients. The lawyers get paid regardless of who wins or loses. The insurance companies need the occasional big payouts to justify the high premiums. They can adjust these premiums to make sure they will profit over time. For us doctors, the system doesn't really think we are doing anything wrong; we are almost always allowed to keep practicing through the whole process and afterward. We are still needed, and the insurance cost is just passed along to the patient.

We doctors may pay a little in psychotherapy or ulcer treatment, but the patients pay the most in inflated fees, a subtle doctor/patient barrier, and overly cautious medical care.

A more pleasant story related to the uterus involved the more recent case of young pregnant lady. She was about twelve weeks along and having pelvic pain. It was episodic and intense. Normally this would point towards the pregnancy being the problem, but my exam pointed more to the bladder.

"How long has it been since you've peed?" Since last night.

A foley catheter proved my suspicions of urinary retention when she had complete relief of her symptoms as the urine could now flow through the catheter and into a bag. The ultrasound techs would have loved this full bladder, and I wanted a good ultrasound, but the patient was too miserable to wait, so we had to empty it.

Hmmm, this was odd. I didn't recall ever hearing about or seeing a young woman in early pregnancy on no medications with urinary retention. I consulted Dr. Google with "pregnancy, urinary retention." About four results down, I saw "Uterine Incarceration." That rang no bells and sounded interesting. A little reading later and "Bing!" This looked promising. The radiologist agreed when he called with the ultrasound report. The fetus was fine, but the uterus was retroverted; he thought incarceration was definitely a possibility.

This was certainly over my head, so I telephoned the patient's OB and laid out the story.

"It can't be *that*, it's super rare," she said and agreed to see the patient soon.

The patient was now without any symptoms. I sent her and her catheter to the OB the next day. I was reminded of her a week or so later, when the OB called me excitedly.

"You were right, it was incarcerated! I popped it back into place this morning," she said.

There are two things remarkable about this story. The most remarkable of the two is that a non-ED doctor specialist made a special call just to tell me I was right. I have never had that happen. I am hoping that it is not because I am never right.

Dr. Google's assistance is the other remarkable thing. I find her most helpful when looking for answers to odd combinations of symptoms or signs. You do need extensive training to avoid being misled.

I have been talking a lot about cases of young women. If you are losing interest in that demographic, I have one brief story about a much older woman. This elderly lady had been transferred in because the small hospital that sent her to us felt she needed a surgeon. They were right.

The surgeon was already in the hospital that night and showed up just minutes after she arrived.

"I don't know about this. I doubt this lady will survive based on what the other hospital told me," the surgeon said.

We walked into the room together. The little old lady was in profound shock. She was frail and thin, but her abdomen was swollen like a double-sized watermelon. Her overall silhouette was that of pregnant teenager at term. The size and tightness of her abdomen was giving her difficulties with breathing. Her belly was very hard. On palpation, it felt precisely like pushing your fingers down on a mouse pad on a desk. Go ahead, push on one: it gives three millimeters then stops, hard as a board. That was this lady's abdomen.

The surgeon was concerned that she would die if he operated or if he didn't. He thought the intestines might just bubble out when he started his incision. Once decompressed, he thought the used-up blood in her legs would be able to get back into circulation and kill her from the toxins in it. Abdominal Compartment Syndrome is the name of this condition.

He is a very good surgeon. Competent and brave and working hard to save lives. He was right that it was too late to save this woman. Her intestines did bulge out through his cut, and the recirculating blood did kill her. It is a travesty that the statistics of ranking surgeons by case mortality rates penalizes them for taking the hard cases.

Wake up! Abrupt tone change ahead. Thank goodness. This next patient was very young and did not look pregnant. That doesn't mean that something did not need delivering.

"Don't worry, we doctors see everything and nothing bothers us." I was doing my best to calm this obviously uncomfortable, but not obviously ill, young lady. Her complaint was an odor, and she was embarrassed. I wanted to decrease her discomfort, because the exam to come would be uncomfortable enough.

In my experience, in delicate situations, it is very important that the caregiver is comfortable and relaxed. (Awkward is extremely contagious.) Some are very cold or clinical, others are very warm and friendly. I usually shoot for cheerful and matter of fact, a "this is no big deal" approach, on the chatty side.

You will have to find a style that fits your personality. It works better if your chosen style aligns closely with the real you. Technical-clinical doesn't work well for me. "I will now palpate the left adnexa[26]," is not my style, but it may be best for you.

You also should be prepared to adjust significantly between patients. This adjustment is easier if you are already acting close to *yourself.* It's easier to keep track of where you're going if you know where you started.

Anyway, in this case, I was hard at work acting like I was not having to work hard. I could tell the situation had made the woman very self-conscious.

I carefully began inserting the speculum in the young woman who all the while kept apologizing for the odor she came to be treated for. I had noticed no odor, and likely said so (although you can be sure I was trying not to notice).

Medical Pearl: Do not just put a glob of lubricant on the top of the speculum—smear it all over.

In continued attempts to minimize her embarrassment, I tried an "it could be worse" maneuver and mentioned others I had found to be in a more difficult situation:

"The only thing that bothers us is forgotten tampons. They smell so horrible. It is a unique smell that we can diagnose a hundred feet away."

As you should foresee, having read this far along in the book, her forgotten tampon brazenly appeared when I opened up the positioned speculum. My quick retrieval and covering the object as I placed it in the trash did not prevent the odor from quickly filling the room and beyond.

I do not recall the rest of the conversation, but I would have had my work cut out for me to smooth the awkwardness I created out of thin air.

Watching what you say is clearly very important. Control everything else you can in a situation, because you often can't

---

[26] I have always doubted that this helps much since "adnexa" (the area around your tubes and ovaries) doesn't really tell the typical patient what you are going to do next.

control a lot. You can at least try to control yourself. Of course, if you get your emotions to submit, you can still easily shoot yourself in your foot with your choice of words. I have some tricks you can do to control your feelings and responses to those.

Learn to avoid bursting out in laughter, making sudden exclamations ("OMG," etc.), or betraying facial expressions that provoke. Instead, deliberately convey whatever emotion is most advantageous for the situation at hand. The difference can sometimes be a question of life or death, especially if patient cooperation is vital.

Odors can be a challenge. I breathe slowly and gently; laminar flow is the key, since your nose is most effective (bad in this case) with turbulence in the nasal cavity. This seems to help me, but I am just guessing about the mechanism here. If the opportunity is there, you can really improve your experience (and therefore your patient's) by not breathing.

Breathing is actually overrated. It is not necessary for the practice of much of medicine. I have been taught numerous times to hold my breath while intubating (I never did this. I use other ways to keep track of time.)

Armed with the foreknowledge of a future odor, I have numerous times treated patients without ever breathing in their room. The priceless foreknowledge will be in the form of a helpful nurse saying, "Get some benzoin and a mask," or a descriptive triage note, "Family made patient come due to the smell."

This is my simplest technique for not breathing: Hyperventilate a few seconds, then pop briskly in the room, while knocking on the door, opening the door, and rubbing hand sanitizer all simultaneously:

"Hello, I'm Doctor McAnonymous, what's the problem in here?" Note that you may substitute something more professional here, but make it brief. Then, you hopefully get brief answers. You are at the mercy of the patient's verbal style here. With a non-verbose historian, I can ask a couple of questions and hear a couple of answers, then:

"Excuse me for a minute." Now I step out, take a deep breath, then go back in.

"So how long has this been draining?" Listen, step back out, and so on.

It may take four or five trips, but I can get a reasonable history and exam and never show anything but a pleasant expression.

Also, if you are walking through an ED and think you smell food, stop breathing. Otherwise, you will soon discover it is not food and will be victimized by some bad odor.

There are women who want to attract a lot of attention, and some of them know how to do so. A related fact is that the average male EMS is a real man, and there are predictable ways to gain his attention. The following illustrates my point.

The EMS radio buzzed to life, and the EMS voice croaked in a slightly higher pitch than his usual. His excitement added an extra rapidity to his call:

"A dancer fell on her head from a pole, we got her spinal packaged, BP 120/80, Pulse 100, Respirations 20, ETA[27] five minutes!" On arrival, even strapped to a backboard, this woman was able to attract attention, and we had an extra hand or two helping with moving her over to the bed.

The unfortunate dancer was wearing a bright and patriotic red, white and blue bikini. I say unfortunate, but she was in no real distress, and we were just mildly concerned about her neck

[27] Estimated Time of Arrival. "five minutes" means zero to fifty minutes.

pain. Although she fell several feet onto her head, she sustained no injuries.

My earlier remark about EMS men requires some further comment. These guys fit the stereotype of real men that has been held throughout most of recorded history. They are tough, strong, masculine first responders. Many of them are firemen also, well-built and in uniforms, thus almost every woman's dream (at least when she is at her most fertile time of the month, according to some study; women pick the more bookish types when not fertile).

There are, of course, lots of exceptions. There are also, of course, many female EMS, however I will not mention them out of spite, due to a gas station prank I will detail later.

On one occasion, a nurse and I discovered an insight regarding the "First Responder" concept. This male nurse (male nurses are highly trained and valued professional healthcare heroes) was a friend. He and I were headed towards the family room when two burly men burst out of the room in a real fistfight.

These two were hitting, grappling, then hitting again. This was not a friendly sibling fight, but a smacking fist event with two contenders really trying to hurt the other. My friend and I slid a little to the side so we could observe the action around the corner for a bit, unseen ourselves.

Was this going to escalate? Are more combatants about to emerge? Are there any weapons involved? The nurse and I contemplated these and other questions as we considered our response. Our "response" starts with a little "r" because:

The First Responder came up from our rear. He ran past us, not acknowledging our existence, and plowed headlong into the two gladiators, pushing them apart and ending the fight. Fascinating. We were impressed.

That is where I learned what it takes to be a real First Responder. A type of concern for others that so dwarfs self-concern that there is little or no hesitation in being the first to help. There is no paralysis of fear, just action. No pause for cautious reflection, just Go! I hesitate to suggest that on some occasions their bravery may be due, in part, to a relative deficit of common sense, because we all would be lost without the First Responder.

We would be lost . . . and a lot of nurses would be lonely. The average male EMS is a destabilizing social force. The female EMS may be a heroic First Responder when not engaged in pranking doctors. However, she generally does not cause similar social upheavals within an emergency department.

Even with liberal application of the "not-all-of-them" caveat, it should still be concluded that EMS should not be left unobserved among female nurses for long periods. Numerous illicit liaisons have resulted when a diligent watch was not kept.

In a related topic, I would like to mention that I think that it is unlikely that I am hideous. My desirability can be proven by the fact that I have fathered two children in only thirty-seven years of marriage. There is also the testimony of the soon-to-be-discussed psychotic girl surrounded by police as well as the elderly woman who shot herself twice. I consider the nurse who called me "Dr. Unibrow" to be an outlier.

Still, I feel somewhat underappreciated due to the fact that I have never been pursued by any females about the hospital. This lack of attention was even present during the brief season in our institution's history when our executives were regularly getting waylaid by intrigues, and our hospital motto was something like, "Pursue Your Healthy Coworker."

That said, I do not report any of the EMS/Nurse connections out of jealousy, I am only reporting a persistent, destabilizing situation. EMS and other uniformed male First Responders have contributed a disproportionate amount to the turmoil of workplace romance, workplace breakups, as well as family breakups. Particular situations are often stabilized by more permanent liaisons between the nursing and EMS staff, with a higher-than-expected rate of marriage between the two departments.

I once walked down the hall of the ED, just one of the halls, and passed eight pregnant nurses. There is also a charge nurse who is one shy of that many pregnancies herself. Many of those children will grow up to look like pictures on the local volunteer fire department calendar (that septo-mom nurse's husband is a soldier, a First Responder subspecies).

You Can't Win

The young lady in 18B did not seem happy. She was reclining quietly with several family members standing about. Her story was that she felt very weak after having had surgery that morning. It was now around eight p.m. The surgery was an exploratory laparoscopy [28] performed by a gynecologist in search of a cause for her chronic pelvic pain.

She looked pale, and had some mild abdominal tenderness, but otherwise seemed fine. She looked like a typical post-op patient. An hour later, her CBC[29] showed a mild anemia. It was time to discuss her with the surgeon. They usually like to keep close tabs on their handiwork.

"Hello Dr. M—, this Dr. McAnonymous. I have Miss B. here. She feels very weak, has a slightly tender abdomen, no more than I would expect. Her hemoglobin is X, and she . . ."

"She's fine, send her home," he interrupted. He knew all about her, she had no real problems, her surgery was routine. "It was just a lap, I didn't do anything."

---

[28] Opening up the belly and looking for problems that can't be diagnosed some less brutal way.

[29] Complete Blood Count. A battery of tests which examine many aspects of blood.

I went back to the room and relayed the surgeon's plan.

The family was not interested in his plan. The patient was puny-feeling enough to just lie there listening. "She's not always this pale!" was the slightly concerned family's next parry.

"Audrey, I need Dr. M— on the phone again."

"So Dr. M—, I talked to the family, but they are reluctant to take her home. They also say she's not usually this pale and has changed since the surgery."

"She's always pale, give her some pain medicine and send her home!"

I knew this was not going to fly. The next step is to put your foot down, stand your ground and get the right thing done for the patient. However, surgeons are by no means pushovers. Things can get very ugly.

As the passive-aggressive sort, I wanted to avoid a fight. However, I still had a plan. To explain, I will need to lay some groundwork first.

It is extremely common for patients or families to push for unreasonable admissions. It is also common, but less so, for physicians to push for unreasonable discharges. Confrontation of one or the other side is sometimes necessary for the safety of all.

Sometimes the issues are so clear, or the stakes are so high, or the time is so short, that you have to immediately fight. More commonly, things are not so clear, who knows who is right, and a less confrontational approach is reasonable.

In this case, I went for the longer game. After discussion with the family and patient, I just kept her in the ED for a couple of hours. I gave her some fluids and repeated her CBC.

"Audrey, I need you to page Dr. M— again!"

"Sorry to bother you again," I said. Note that it is important to speak in such a manner in almost all situations, with pleasantries or apologies, etc. For example, I was not really sorry. I was just doing my job and he was doing his. This type of talk may not truly represent the situation or positions of those involved, but it helps preserve civilization.

"She feels no better, and her hemoglobin has dropped a point," I informed him.

"McAnonymous? Didn't you give her fluids? That's why her hemoglobin dropped. I just did an exploratory laparoscopy; I didn't really do anything. Send her home!" His tone was firm.

This was unexpected. He was possibly right about the fluids, but I hadn't given her *that* much saline, and it seemed a little gutsy of him to keep pushing. This patient must have had a long history of being a problem for him. I was not yet defeated.

The woman was not obviously in danger, but she did not feel good. I did not feel happy sending her home with abdominal tenderness, pallor, weakness and recent abdominal surgery, so I did what is my specialty—nothing. Well, sort of nothing. I let her sleep in 18B and kept her monitored the rest of the night. The family was also OK with this "overnight observation."

She never showed any deterioration, and I strategically picked a time to repeat her CBC so that the results would come back in time before the surgeon got busy, but as late as possible to make the test either more reassuring or more concerning.

It was the latter. She had dropped a couple more points of hemoglobin. Her abdomen was still tender, she hadn't changed for better or worse to appearances, but her hemoglobin was telling another story.

"Audrey! I need Dr. M—!" I do not recall this particular interaction, but any of our clerks would likely have rolled their eyes, cursed, or thrown something at me to indicate their displeasure at calling the same person repeatedly.

"Her hemoglobin has dropped to seven," I said. Surely, I had won.

"Well, McAnonymous, I would have admitted her the first time you called, if I'd known you were going to keep her all night!" He somehow kept the pecking order intact, with me clearly towards the bottom. For my part, the OB/GYN was on the case, the family was happy, and the patient wasn't complaining. It was a win-win-win.

Of course, you can't actually win, certainly not three times. Dr. M— made one last pass for a touchdown with his "Hail Mary" the next day.

"McAnonymous! It was just a little bleeder! She was just bleeding, and all I had to do was tie it off!" He acted like his mistake was mine. He used a tone of voice calculated to turn my win, my saving him of having a potentially disastrous surgical complication, into a loss. I was impressed.

I have also noticed that talent for never admitting that you are wrong in other situations. I remember a doctor on the phone who vociferously pushed for "Plan A." He was loud and bellicose. In person this doctor continued to berate me in a combative manner, pushing hard for "Plan B." He seemed totally unaware that he was contradicting himself in content. Incoherence of thought had been replaced by a coherence of style. I was intrigued by this behavior and began noticing it scattered around the place.

Along the same lines, I once treated a pregnant auto accident patient. She had a badly fractured ankle, with bones protruding through the skin, with the addition of a dislocation. She was also far along in her pregnancy and having periodic contractions with hints of issues with the baby. Having no worse injuries, she needed to be delivered.

With skill beyond an absolute beginner, I quickly reduced her ankle to protect its blood supply, cover the exposed bone, and relieve some of her suffering. I splinted the now better-looking ankle, and the OB took her upstairs for a c-section. It's a win!

Wrong, of course. A few days later, a prominent orthopedist called me to a quiet place in the hall. The red rose in his face and his veins bulged as if a nurse had misplaced a tourniquet around his neck. He began a series of, "Why did you do this?" and "Why did you do that?"

After my fourth reasonable answer, his appearance immediately changed to normal and he said, "OK." That was it. His appearance of anger seemed to be a front. Not only had he mastered the art of hiding his emotions, he could also generate them at will! I was impressed.

The Case of the Blood-Bloated Belly

Being a woman typically means developing a close connection with blood. Blood is everywhere in the female world and causes a number of issues. Most of the time in the ED, "bleeding" means hormonal or pregnancy issues. Of course, rules are made to make you miss the important exceptions.

This woman was not bleeding visibly, but she was bleeding. She was maybe forty years old with a very firm, distended, thirty-seven-week-sized abdomen. She was in profound shock. Her mentation was decreased, she was extremely pale, her pulse was fast, and her blood pressure was low. There was some hope when my femoral trauma line insertion was quick, and we were able to rapidly give her fluids and blood through that very large bore line as well as her peripheral IVs.

"Abruptio placenta!" [30] were the words I used when negotiating with the ultrasound tech regarding her need to drag her machine across the hospital for an ultrasound. It was a big deal then to move the large, "ancient" machines, and I had never seen one in the ED.

"She's way too unstable to move," was also part of my negotiation, and it worked.

---

[30] A dread condition where the placenta separates early and lots of blood can accumulate in the space.

Fortunately, the "unstable" was unstable and the patient became more stable with the treatment. Her rock hard, bulging, tender belly exam was consistent with an abruption, and I really hadn't entertained another diagnosis until the ultrasound.

On the screen appeared a big black soccer ball. This deep black on the ultrasound meant that it was fluid. That would be blood based on the patient's appearance. The tech pointed out the normal uterus and adnexa, and it was apparent that this was not an abruption. It was not an ovarian cyst or one of those huge benign ovarian tumors (you should Google-image search these).

The lady's physical parameters had improved, but she was still not alert. It was hard to leave the OB/GYN paradigm, but I decided the best person to call was the general surgeon.

I was on the money with that call.

"I don't know what that is either, we'll just have to take her up and see," was his diagnosis and plan.

This kindly, competent, tall, good-looking (I'm no expert), older surgeon took this barely stable patient off my hands. Note: It is such a relief to us ED guys when these types of patients leave the department. That is our little victory. We get them back from the brink of death (or beyond), and they make it upstairs.

Upstairs? What happened next? You will notice how few of my stories give you the full story. That's because I don't remember, or I never found out. It's not that I don't care, it's just that those patients are so quickly replaced with other new patients that there is no time to linger. Only rarely do I get the real ending.

I did in the case of this woman who bled to almost-death. The surgeon came back down with the news.

He said, "It was a bleeding inferior epigastric artery. An aneurysm or tear or something. She just filled her belly wall with blood. I just tied it off. She's fine."

Assorted Cases

Case 1

I saw an exceptionally sullen woman. I had seen her in past visits depressed or enraged or even manic. I do not recall what had disturbed her that day, but it must have been something huge.

She stabbed an ice pick straight into her chest, right towards her heart. The handle wobbled visibly in synchronized time with her pulse.

She seemed to be unharmed. I do not think that was her intended outcome, because she also stuck a serrated steak knife into her chest.

This looked more painful, but less dangerous due to its tangential trajectory that appeared to not enter beyond the ribs.

We were very careful not to disturb the disturbed woman's ice pick as the trauma surgeon took her upstairs. On the OR table, with tools out and ready, he removed the ice pick, and nothing happened.

Case 2

The young man, in his late teens, was lying in the unit. He had overdosed on some antibiotics but would be fine. As his mom and I walked up to the foot of the bed, he vomited a shiny jet-black waterfall of activated charcoal. It immediately coated his chin and chest.

The mother was not calm about the aesthetics of the situation. It certainly looked straight from some horror movie, but the patient was unharmed.

Before this hospitalization, I had seen this patient often over the past few months. He was present at all his teen girlfriend's prenatal OB care visits. He also stayed with her throughout the delivery. I asked him why he made the suicide attempt.

"On the night of delivery, she told me I wasn't the father," he said.

Ouch. Being a teen father or not being a teen father can be hard on you.

Case 3

This occurred in the late 1980s. My family practice clinic patient was seventy-four years old. Her tests confirmed that she had newly acquired syphilis. I carefully prepared her and gave her my diagnosis.

"Whew, I thought you was gonna tell me I got AIDS."

Case 4

When the surgeon came to treat the abdominal compartment syndrome lady, I talked about how us sheepfarmers can "pop" the dangerously bloated bellies of sheep. Could something similar be done here? I got to test this idea many years later when I ran across another of these cases.

This was a young, developmentally delayed man with a huge rock-hard abdomen. He coded within minutes of arrival. Ventilation was very difficult. After a brief discussion, my colleague and I decided on a last-ditch maneuver. We could not make him worse than the dead that he was. We both inserted large needles into his abdomen, aiming for the most tympanitic areas. The rush of foul gas was promising, but the pressure in his abdomen was not relieved enough to prevent its deadly effects and he did not regain a pulse.

6
Children

Some ED clinicians hate taking care of children. I know why. Their conditions are frequently tricky to diagnose, with your options of deathly ill and perfectly healthy ping-ponging back and forth with rapidity and in a maddeningly random pattern. The ones you think are sick end up being fine and the ones you think are fine end up being sick. The science of medicine isn't always quite up to the task.

At first, all the negative (those are good) workups really wear you down. Over time, the few positive (those are bad) ones sprinkled along will keep you motivated. There are bad diseases out there.

Others do not like dealing with worried or demanding parents. The discussions are often long and contentious, with the subject matter often involving old wives' tales or unreasonable fears. There are debates with Dr. Google.

For me, the rewards outweigh the penalties. I like the laughing children and the young mothers. I try extra hard to get the kids laughing or smiling. This gaiety has frequently changed the course of my own disposition made dark by the prior patient or the situation in the room next door.

I get fatigued by too many old patients with belly pain or chest pain in succession and crave some variety. The babies and children who are not very sick, for the most part, are enlivening.

I almost always begin such visits with playing. Unless there is reason to believe a deadly serious illness is at hand, I will peer around the door, make faces, and act goofy. The mother typically watches the child for a response. When the child begins to smile or play, the mom now relaxes. The child's smile reassures her (and me) to a significant degree.

I have learned a couple of coin tricks (they are astounding!) and these work magic in gaining a child's trust and getting them to lower their guard. A child's guarded stance may imitate the appearance of illness, so it is nice for both me and mom to see it melt away.

I do these tricks so often that occasionally a child will remember it from a prior visit and spoil it. I always show them how it works, to help teach some healthy skeptical thinking.

For years I had great success stopping infants or toddlers from crying by making a loud popping noise. They would frequently become attentive to me and laugh. I always thought it was the noise, until one day I saw myself in the mirror. I looked like an overhyped clown, with wildly raised eyebrows and an exaggerated, induced overbite. All those years, the children were laughing *at* me.

Another trick I use to melt the ice is to act like an idiot. Dozens of nurses would say that this is easy for me, as I am a natural, authentic idiot. Nurses are mean. Regardless, young toddlers to young teens will lose their reserve and be themselves if they are sure they are superior to you.

"How old are you?" The little girl holds up four fingers. I would like to hear her talk because her mom has indicated a complaint is related to her airway. Sullen silence will hamper my investigation.

"Wow, you're two years old?" The little eyebrows shoot me a scowl, the four fingers are pushed in my direction. I keep making wrong guesses as the child tries to avoid words by more and more overt finger displays.

"Ten? One? Forty?"

The child's increasingly desperate attempts to communicate the number four by using facial expressions and hand gestures will eventually explode into a soft, slightly hoarse, exasperated: "Four! I'm four years old, almost five."

And now we're off. The child answers questions or makes fun of my shoe covers or guesses wrong regarding my magic tricks. The relief is palpable in the adults in the room.

It's all an act, I'm not an idiot. The nurses are wrong. However, I can be very convincing. I found myself once in the exact setting noted above.

The little girl was seated on the bed with her father standing nearby. Her vitals and pulse ox were normal, and her overall appearance was normal. The complaint was "Cough, can't breathe," so I desperately needed one more hint.

I started my "misunderstand-the-finger routine." When I got to about the third wrong "guess," the father grabbed my arm.

"You idiot! Take care of my daughter! She can't breathe, what are you doing?"

I stepped around the corner with him and explained the situation and my goals. He quickly calmed down (not a given) and joined in as I redeployed the method with the desired results, a croupy "Four!"

That is the only exception I recall. If the parents were muttering under their breaths, I have been blissfully unaware.

It is possible I am aided by unusually comic face. Perhaps surprisingly, I have not had trouble gaining the parents' real trust when the situation does prove to be serious. Humor seems to create some emotional trust. Since the odds are in your favor, I suggest expending the effort to begin with a lighter approach.

Of course, you have to make sure you can quickly and convincingly switch gears to "trained professional" if something serious is turning up. There are times it is important to appear intelligent, but that is less often than you think.

Other idiotic things I have done in the name of caring for children is poke myself with needles to prove it's "no big deal." Right. I also let a child pull off his own damaged fingernail (I had already numbed his whole finger) because he was afraid to let me do it. I stabilized things and undermined the nail while he actually pulled it off. I am not sure why that made it easier for him, but it did.

Parental Pearl: The hinge side of doors is much more hazardous than the closing side. Many children learn this the hard way.

I like to mostly talk to the child instead of the adults whenever possible. You have to work to get some parents to give their child the floor. You also can do this so that mom actually knows you are talking to her. Tell the child about dosages, follow-up, etc. It's all friend-building communication in the child's mind.

It's easier to get the child to talk if you don't talk about *them* so much. Ask about their stuffed dog (call it a cat to spur conversation) or princess toy ("That's not Ariel!"). I sometimes go on a brief monologue about my own pets, or shoes, anything that doesn't force the child to be self-conscious.

Even though they are fun, I can recall one good reason that there are those who don't like to treat children—the stakes are very high. Also, the odds are not always in your favor.

Why You Should Be Afraid of Children

She may have been the first patient I saw on my night shift. The mom was clearly worried. "A child in our neighborhood had meningitis just a month ago, and it started in his knee." Her daughter was complaining of knee pain today.

The eleven-year-old girl's right knee looked fine. It was not swollen or discolored. There was no history of trauma unless you counted her walking around at an amusement park all day before coming to the ED. All of her vital signs were normal; she had no fever.

The first hint of a problem was a grimace when I moved her knee. Grimaces are pretty useful indicators in children. The rest of her exam was normal, including her neck. I demonstrated the flexing neck to her mother to reassure her regarding meningitis.

I was not too concerned about that dread disease, but I was concerned enough about a potential knee infection to order labs. Sticking a child for labs is a big enough deal to justify careful consideration. I was concerned enough to do the fairly easy labs, but not enough to tap the knee or call a consultant yet.

I was treating other patients while waiting for the lab results. The nurse interrupted to inform me that the mom had spotted a rash. I had discussed the lack of any rash on my exam with the mother, so I was curious to see what she was seeing.

On the girl's knee was a small purple dot, raised slightly and maybe three millimeters in diameter. I pressed it and it did not blanch. That was not good. The dreaded purpura lesion.[31]

Now I joined the mother in being definitely worried, but I still was not worried about what she was worried about. Based on the rash, I was really worried about some horrible joint infection and sepsis. I immediately ordered large doses of antibiotics and IV fluids.

Her CBC showed a slightly low white blood cell count. Her skin began to show more spots. These were little blood vessels bursting under her skin. I called the admitting pediatric resident, and he responded quickly. By the time she made it to the PICU she was covered in purple patches and acting lethargic.

The next morning, I visited upstairs. Several family members were sitting along a wall, looking appropriately serious. The child was now intubated, fully plugged in to the ICU apparatus. The rash had expanded and become confluent,

[31] Purple lesions caused by bursting tiny blood vessels. Potentially ominous signs when associated with infections.

and now the girl was completely purple. The next day she was dead. It was determined that fulminant meningococcemia was the cause.

Two years later I was delivered the letter. "Failure to diagnose meningitis, failure to perform an LP," and "abandonment of patient" were a couple of the reasons stated for the lawsuit. "Murder" was buried deeper down in the paperwork.

This did not surprise me exactly, especially since my experience as a resident, but it certainly gave me a shock. My overall mood dampened, my enthusiasm for patient care lessened, and I felt a little more of a wall between the world of medicine and myself.

Nothing else occurred for a while. I had a couple of meetings with my new company-assigned lawyer. The machinery of the lawsuit dragged on slowly enough that I occasionally had time to forget all about it. As soon as I was my old self, another letter would arrive, and pull me back to a new, less-bright reality. I eventually accumulated a two-foot-tall stack of letters and paperwork.

The affair hung over me like a cloud, both the lawsuit and the tragedy. From my perspective, I had done nothing wrong and was correctly aggressive when there was enough reason to be. I listened hard to the mother and addressed her concerns up front. I rushed to the bedside when the mom spotted the rash. At the time, she didn't indicate any concerns regarding my care.

I could understand that the mother would think I should have given antibiotics right when she mentioned "meningitis." I thought it reasonable that the mother would raise questions or that even some peer review process should occur.

However, the accusations of "abandonment" and "murder"? I was livid at the doctor who had given his expert opinion on the case. It was like he only half-read the chart. I did not fail to diagnose meningitis; she didn't have it. There was even a timely, and normal, LP done after admission.

"Abandonment?" I was in the department the whole time and went into the room numerous times.

"Murder?" That certainly seems personal, even when the chummy lawyers say it's not.

I treated a couple of children with severe infections as the suit dragged on. I even treated a child member of the suing lawyer's family. If anyone really thought I was guilty of murder, why didn't they call the police? Why should I still be allowed to treat patients? I can't say I didn't lose some self-confidence in the ordeal, but not much changed because I was already pretty self-critical. Most doctors are, even if they hide it well.

The deposition was an impressive and intimidating affair. There was a long table. I sat at the head, three or four lawyers sat down each side. A stenographer sat nearby. In case she missed anything, a tape recorder and a video recorder was set up and aimed at me.

I do not recall a single question. I remember my lawyer objecting to some question about a book. I remember the hospital's lawyer pop up from his dozing position to address a question that veered towards his territory, before he slumped back to the appearance of sleep. I was impressed.

The lawyers never (possibly intentionally) indicated that they comprehended the meanings of meningitis, meningococcal disease or meningococcemia. They butchered these words ferociously.

There was also some confusion about the likelihood of the child's death. Meningococcal meningitis had "only" a twenty percent death rate, whereas meningococcal sepsis without meningitis had a worse, eighty percent death rate. The child had the worse of the two. Whether I was more likely to save her or more likely to lose her as a patient hung in the balance of that confusion.

I do recall the sensation of having that lawyer on my side. He was only on my side; there was no possibility that the opposing lawyer was right. I live and breathe in the fuzzy world of grey and he protected me from his sharp-edged black-and-white world.

In an early meeting with just my lawyer, when discussing the details of the case, I said, "Things went pretty well." He cut me off with his hand and his eyes.

"I know you are just referring to your medical care, how the orders were getting done, IVs and the rest, but all they will say is: 'What? The girl died? Is that your idea of going well?' Just use some different words."

The opposing lawyer was even more diabolical than expected. During the deposition, he began his attack.

"So, Dr. McAnonymous, this patient, you diagnosed her with 'viral syndrome?'" he asked innocently. But was that a sneer? Whatever his tone, it was clearly malevolent.

"Uhm, no sir, I diagnosed her with 'severe sepsis.'" I was recalling my lawyer's instructions to not let them annoy me or bait me into acting arrogant.

"My chart says 'viral syndrome,'" the lawyer pressed.

"No sir." I pointed, "Right here: 'severe sepsis.'"

"Well, on my chart, it says 'viral syndrome.'" He pointed about a third of the way up the chart at those words listed under the differential diagnosis.

"No, that is under the differential diagnosis," I offered, thinking maybe he was truly confused.

"So, you are saying you did not diagnosis 'viral syndrome' even though it is plainly in the chart?" That was surely a sneer.

"No! That was a part of the differential diagnosis, that was not my final diagnosis." I was firm.

"OK, Doctor. We'll let that slide for now." He said this with a smirk and a look about the room, masterfully insinuating I was hiding something. Diabolically clever. I was again impressed by a lawyer. And I despised this whole process that obscures more than it uncovers.

I really admired and felt grateful for my own, company-supplied lawyer (he was costing them a bundle). He even helped me get a loan.

"Are you being sued?" The young clerk asked in a tired refrain during my remortgaging attempt.

My "Yes" clearly startled her.

"Umm, I'll be right back." She came back with the news that my loan couldn't go forward until I got a letter from my lawyer.

My lawyer wrote, "Dr. McAnonymous cannot possibly lose this lawsuit. He did nothing wrong and will win. Even if he did somehow lose, this could not possibly affect his ability to pay off a loan." That was the gist of it, and that was all it took to refinance my house, even as it felt like it was crumbling around me.

The suit limped along in a cycle. The forgetting all about it, then the deflating items in the mailbox, then forgetting again lasted about two years.

This all ended one day when the suing lawyer died. No one else was willing to continue it, so the suit was dropped. It was over for me. I doubt the ordeal helped the family of the child at all. Maybe the mom got some answers, but I doubt it.

One thing that probably added to the mother's grief was guilt that she should have pushed harder, done something, because she *knew* her daughter had meningitis. I often tell families of patients who just died things like, "No, if you had come yesterday when he first had chest pain, it wouldn't have made a difference." Or, "There's nothing more you could have done. You told us he was sick, and we worked hard on him." There is no sense adding the burden of guilt on top of grief.

For a year after the suit was dropped, I was still intermittently livid at the doctor who first reviewed my case and considered countersuing, but wiser parts of my brain were too lazy to pursue such justice. I saw the last name of the little girl's family pop up in the ED over the years, but I never saw (or recognized[32]) the mother again, and none of those with the family name seemed to recognize me. Seeing the name in print or on a screen always got my attention.

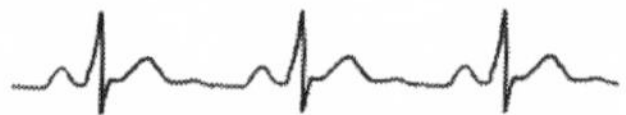

Children hit us emotionally way more than most patients. If I want to feel sad, I have an album of mental images I can scroll through: The little eight-year-old with long black hair that I watched walk all the way across the ED to room 3C; she was dead of some hemorrhagic pneumonia the next day. The little boy with a prolonged seizure who never woke up and died of some encephalitis (room 3A); Numerous beaten-to-death or shaken-to-death or slashed-to-death infants and children. I can recall that I have tried to save, too late, around fifty stiffening dolls of babies who died in their cribs. I see them as faded framed pictures on a shelf in my mind. I hear faint echos of the wails of mothers.

I can remember a full thirty years later the sixteen-year-old who died of meningitis; our attempts at treatment and a precise diagnosis were hampered by the hierarchy of academic medicine and the resident's inability to obtain an LP.[33] She would likely have died anyway, but . . .

It is crucial to realize the other world of laughing, singing happiness is just a curtain's width away from the above horrors. You cannot stay on one side of the curtain for too long. Medicine's greatest cure for its own practitioners is that it

---

[32] People say, "I never forget a face." How would they know? It's not like they would remember names and not be able to picture the person. They just forgot both.

[33] Lumbar Puncture. Not always easy to do.

forces you to move on. New compelling responsibilities push you back on a forward path.

The little boy had a stab wound right over his heart. He was around nine. He said he fell on the pocketknife and it went all the way in. The story was that he was alone, but we were still suspicious he was covering for someone.

Like most stab wounds, serious or not, not much active bleeding was to be seen, just a minor-looking laceration oozing a little blood. Internal bleeding is the killer, and, in this case, his very low blood pressure made us suspicious more was going on than met the eye.

Soon, he got even more pale and a little lethargic. His breath sounds were good bilaterally, although an asymmetry here would signal a pneumothorax that I could treat. No such luck.

We got IVs in him and gave him more oxygen as he hovered on the brink. A nurse prodded, "Do something." What was there for me to do?

This was one of those really scary cases for me. If the child truly crashed and coded, the protocols were clear, and I couldn't make him worse. I might be hyped-up and energized, but I wouldn't likely be *afraid* to take care of him if he coded.

However, this little boy scared me. He still had lots of life in him, and I could make him worse by something I did, or something I didn't do. Only one nurse said it, but I could feel the others wanting me to fix him.

His chest x-ray was normal. Did his heart sound muffled? I recalled the adult who had the blood-clotted cardiac tamponade, and this was my greatest suspicion. I got some things in preparation, and what did I do?

Nothing but wait. We had already called "Trauma," so real help was on the way. The little boy continued to hover, then he was taken to surgery (I am sure my relief was visible), where the surgeon cut a piece of the pericardium out, preventing accumulating blood from making the heart ineffective. The little boy did fine.

These kinds of cases, with responsibilities thrown at you, force you to dig your way out of any dark corners. You often find some light when things turn out OK. The children can give you even more light when they laugh and play and tease. They will grab your legs or chase you down the hall to offer you some joy.

They let you return the favor by treating them for things that are not scary, that are not life-or-death, but still need to be done. The stakes don't always have to be high for the payoff to be great:

- Get fingers unstuck from a plastic rocking horse (it took saws and tin snips).
- Sew up lots of cuts.
- Get foreign bodies from ears and noses.

Do Not Try to Show Off

It was in the "golden hour" of my shift, only one hour to go! It was after two a.m. Confident of my efficiency and my skill as a "Child Whisperer," I grabbed the resident. "Come check this out."

The complaint read: "Two-year-old, FB in nose." I like foreign bodies and children, and usually cases with the combination of the two. I was looking forward to teaching the resident some tricks and speeding along the ER stay for the young family.

Of course, you cannot win. As I have mentioned. I also may have mentioned that I do not like bad smells. Sometimes we diagnose FBs in noses due to mysterious smells reported by parents, and I noticed this one right away, but it struck me as a little different.

The odd smell was explained when the mother informed me that this precious angel was fond of sculpting little balls of her own stool. "She likes to hide them in her room, and we find them all over the place—little dried balls of stool."

The cherubic face was accessorized by a stool ball that appeared in her left nostril. This was surprisingly hard to remove, with a piecemeal technique involving some interruptions for retching. The smell was horrible, I had to get close to this smell, and the child was not cooperative.

In this next nose incident, you will be reminded of one of my patella patients. This foreign body was a largish bead in the left naris. *Useless Trivia Pearl: No, it is not "nare." "Naris" is the correct singular for "nares." You heard it from me first.*

The plastic bead's cheery color was only fleetingly apparent when the restless toddler breathed a certain way. After a short but serious consideration of the issue at hand, and with extraordinary speed and exquisite timing developed from years of medicine and the husbandry of countless fast and vicious predators (falconry is a hobby of mine), I made my move.

At the precise moment the child made the maneuver that made the bead visible, I trapped it by pressing a finger on the side of the nose, deftly popping it right out. I was impressed.

The mother was not. I was dismissed with a snarky: "I'd have just done it myself if I'd known it was that easy."

Medical Pearl: Nerve hooks can be rotated into the hole of a bead that is wedged in a nose. The super-smooth instruments are less likely to damage mucosa.

As I mentioned earlier, some folks are OK with the children; it's the parents that trouble them. There are lots of ways to make that easier, but the best way is to show that you like them and their child.

Most parents assume you are smart, but amazingly they will think you are withholding some miracle cure because you're annoyed by them, or don't like them, or don't want to expend the resources. *Nice beats smart* in dealing with parents and may save you some meetings over complaints.

Give overly worried mothers credit for caring. Let them know worrying is their job. They're not supposed to know much about medicine—that's your job. It's easier to sell the "no antibiotics" approach, you can get away with making fun of them, and they are less likely to come back in six hours for a second opinion if they feel you liked and understood them.

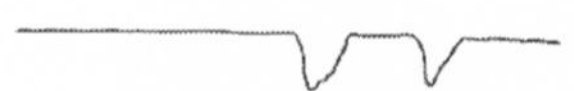

He was two years old when I first encountered him. He met with some horrible accident or genetic abnormality and was already on a ventilator at home. His attentive parents were beyond extremely concerned and reached the point of being abrasively demanding, really bothering the nurses. Other clinicians dreaded treating this family. I didn't mind too much, but I had no pride and tried my hardest to do whatever the mother wanted.

Over the years, I saw this child grow in stature, but not in mental capability. He remained a nearly unresponsive, bedridden, noncommunicative ventilator patient. His mother thought she could detect communication intent in his face and hand squeezing, but I never saw anything convincing. The mother remained hyper-focused; the father left.

The child finally died around age twenty, but he was never really much alive. I hope he wasn't alive enough to suffer greatly all those years.

It is best to tread very carefully around parents of children with rare or significant maladies. These caregivers frequently know more than most doctors do about their child's particular condition, and they will spot you immediately if you try to bluff. It is safest to work hard to assure them that you are listening and concerned. They will forgive you if you say something like:

"Whose syndrome? I don't think I've ever even heard of that one. I may have to do some research on that, but I don't think it will impact us treating his impetigo—I will check and make sure."

It is worth repeating that patients or parents generally assume you are smart enough. They need to be convinced you like them enough, and that you have the time and are attentive enough to give them the treatment they assume exists. In their minds, a cure is available—it's a matter of whether you will give it to them. If no real treatment exists, you really have to prove you care for them and you have to do a lot of talking. The less you have to offer, the more you have to talk, and the faster you have to get them on their way.

One case (it's not exciting—get used to that, the occasional good case will be enough for your job satisfaction over the years) illustrates another important skill: managing a parent's trust in "The System."

But You're a Good Doctor

It is tempting to accept the praise. "You're the first doctor to do anything," or "Finally, someone who knows what they are doing." Do not accept that drink. It has been tampered with, and who knows what will happen to you.

This little infant was transferred to us because he needed surgery for a "strangulated hernia." It was in the wee hours of the morning and we were caught up, so my partner for that shift and I both went in to see this potentially interesting case.

The child had a fever and was grumpy, but did not look deathly ill. He had a several-centimeter-sized, swollen, angry red mass in his right groin. It looked too far down to be a hernia, and a little more careful checking proved to us that it was not a hernia, but a large, infected lymph node (you may recall I have had similar confusion).

Upon us both concluding that this was an infected lymph node, the other doctor stepped back, lowered his eyebrows, and said with some derision, "That's not a hernia!" The mother suddenly became alarmed. I could feel her losing faith in The Process.

I could have led her towards the path of following Us, the good doctors, and leaving the prior, bad doctors. That was a high-risk gambit. If things went south, we would all have gotten sued when caught up in her attempts to extract some justice or vengeance against the "bad" doctors. That path also would put the impossible responsibility on the mom to decide which doctors to listen to.

I suggest a higher path, and better for all concerned. This path calms the mother, minimizes doubt, and smooths the path for future conversations. This approach best helps the little fellow on the bed before us.

"Yeah, we think that may be a large abscess, not a hernia. Don't worry, they did the right thing. They gave him good antibiotics and sent him to the right place. It doesn't really matter which problem it is. At this point, it is a serious problem and we just need to get him a surgeon."

Now, those are calculatedly reassuring words. I threw "serious" in there for a reason. If things go south, I want her to blame the disease, not us doctors. The mother must be able to trust the whole system to some degree. She is entrusting the life of her baby to it, and it is cruel to make her unnecessarily choose between "good" and "bad" doctors. It is more important for her to trust The Process than you as an individual.

I find that in almost all situations, it works better to not throw others under buses, literally and figuratively.

Patients who complain, "My doctor has done nothing," are best treated by pointing out: "Well, maybe, if by 'nothing' you mean this CT scan, these dozens of labs, this referral to GI ... Clearly, your doctor is taking you seriously and checking you out. Just fuss at him if you think he acts tired of you. You're paying him, you're in charge. You just rattle off your symptoms. He will be afraid to miss something important. So am I. I still think your symptoms are from anxiety, but I will repeat some things here. Remember, this is an ED and we are not as equipped to take care of you for this as your regular doctor. Your best bet is to go see your doctor again, just talk to him about all this." Or something like that.

"Ears can become infected quickly. It probably *was* normal when your pediatrician checked two days ago."

Managing emotions are a large part of ED life. Both mine, the patients', and the parents' emotions can help or hurt the whole process. Lots of the time, I engage in a fairly high-risk approach to this.

The young mother sat, holding her baby boy in her lap. He was clearly trying to charm me, a good omen in this world of meningitis. The mother looked anxious as she said, "He hit his head," The smiling head looked up at me, and he bounced with both arms held up to accentuate his embrace of life.

"He was crawling along on the floor, and crawled right into the table leg, hitting his head."

Hearing this while playing with the baby, I threw the first punch: "Ma'am, that is the lamest head injury story I have ever heard."

Her left jab for the knockout was, "He has severe hemophilia."

She won fair and square. I retreated to my corner of the ring. She watched me carefully check the little rascal[34] and then play with him for a few minutes. I think the mother didn't get mad because my playing with the infant conveyed concern and attention that my teasing did not.

Usually, I win these high-stakes bouts. The conditions have to be just right, but sometimes laughing at a mother is the fastest way to a cure. If the baby looks perfect, just repeating the story with emphasis or an eye roll is often enough, e.g., "He fell, from a *fully seated position*?" or "He *sneezed*?" As is noted above, there are caveats, and one must be quick to regroup.

These mothers can tell that I mean them no harm. They are frequently the only adult in the room[35] or even the only adult in the child's life, and their abundance of caution is ultimately borne of a deep and tender love, which is the best reason for the universe to be. If they know you know that, it gets you some credibility.

Assorted Cases

Case 1

I was a resident on duty in the wee hours of the morning. A woman had just delivered a premature baby. It was alive when born, but we did not have the capability then to transport such a young fetus nor to keep one alive.

---

[34] The neuro exam has much power to heal. Checking eye muscle function is very similar to a priestly Sign of the Cross.
[35] Myself excepted—I have to clarify because this is an opportunity for some nurse to say, "Yea, you and the mom in the room, that's one adult."

My job was to pronounce death. Although I came quickly when summoned, death came slowly and couldn't be pronounced for a terribly long time (maybe thirty minutes?). I watched the little baby, with the ten little fingers and tiny toes, almost keep breathing, almost gain a life, then gradually diminish those efforts as it found peace.

Case 2 & 3

I've seen two two-year-old toddlers fall from two-story windows with zero injury (both landed in shrubs).

Case 3 & 4

I have seen two one-year-olds that suffered no harm from vehicles rolling over their heads (soft sand in one case, I don't recall how the other escaped undamaged.)

7

Animals

I love and live with lots of animals. So did the lady who snuck the cat into her ED room in her purse. Many of us like animals, but they certainly cause problems. Hip fractures are commonly enough caused by tripping over pets.

We see lots of head injuries from horses. Frequently these patients are female teen competitive riders. These girls are usually more worried about the horse than they are themselves. It seems horses are just the right height to inflict the maximum damage. If they were shorter, you'd land on your side. If they were taller, you'd land on your feet. Horses are actually sized just right for you to land on your head.

Deer cause lots of wrecks and create lots of patients. My colleague saw several injured patients at once when the deer came through the windshield and started kicking the car's occupants.

Animals add some interest to the ED, and I walk a lot quicker to rooms with animal-related complaints. I always hope they brought the critter in question.

"Bit by squirrel, here for rabies shots." I saw this pop up on the tracking board. Ha ha! Squirrels don't carry rabies. I was going to have fun teasing this person and hearing this story. I walked over to the minor care area where she was seated. She was a calm, middle-aged woman.

"I was working on my roof when the squirrel ran up the ladder and started attacking my legs. I shook it off and it ran away. I climbed down the ladder and back it came. It kept attacking me. I couldn't chase it off. I finally escaped inside."

That was not your typical squirrel bite ("I picked it up and . . ."). Although squirrels don't carry rabies, they can certainly spread it if they are in the throes of the disease. So, she got her rabies shots and not much teasing from me.

Dog bites are, of course, our most popular pet-related complaint. I've sewn up lots of faces and extremities. Some of these were very bad, disfiguring wounds.

My colleague had a patient die from a capnocytophaga infection (pretty word). I peeked my head in the room and saw that the unfortunate lady's arm did not look too bad, with not much swelling and just a few punctures. The week-old bite, however, did a number on her CBC, making her platelets plummet, and she was very septic and beyond hope when she arrived at the ED.

I can recall one truly notable dog-bite case.

Dog Mauling

The woman had just been wheeled into the trauma room, Bed T4. I immediately noticed a mass of strikingly blond, thick curly hair. The pale young woman was partly covered by sheets and lying quietly on the bed. The mass of hair was on the table beside her. That was not good at all. Her monitor looked fine and she was obviously alert, even calm. There were spots of blood everywhere on the linens.

"Hey, I'm Dr M, are you breathing OK?"

"Yes," she answered softly.

The top of her head was a hairless mess of congealed blood and shiny tissue. She had a dog bite mark on every square inch of her pale body. Other than the scalp, the other wounds didn't appear to be particularly bloody or life-threatening, and she was not bleeding briskly even from her scalp.

When the trauma surgeon arrived, he mentioned to her the necessity of transfer for plastic surgery. As he talked to her it was apparent that he thought she was at grave risk of dying and raised the topic of transfusion.

"No transfusion," she interrupted firmly.

"Are you Jehovah's Witness?" somebody asked.

She was, and thus began the coaxing, arguing, cajoling, and multi-person discussions in attempts to get her to accept blood. The surgeon described this in stark terms as a matter of life or death, but she held firm to her convictions.

I thought the surgeon might have been a little pessimistic. Her BP was OK, the bleeding was now controlled, and surely, these days she would be OK.

It turns out that she was playing with her own pit bull with some visiting dog neighbors. She bent over to pick up the ball and the dogs all pounced, mauling her in her own yard.

She was cool, calm, peaceful. I spent some time with her due to the blood discussions and issues regarding a transfer. She was composed and brave.

"You're a bad patient," I teased when she rejected one more argument for blood.

She smiled wryly—my hoped-for effect. Those are the last words I remember saying. There should have been some goodbyes as she headed off to the Big City hospital, but I can't recall them. I wish I remembered some other words, as I was saddened and slightly surprised to hear that she died within the week.

So far, for decades, the sight of that color hair usually recalls her to mind. Years later, that color hair also awakened the memory of another patient. That is a fortunate thing, and you will see why when you read that story in the "Hearts" chapter.

Snake!

Snakebites are more pleasant for me to contemplate. I have never seen a fatality or facial disfiguring. They are rarely a disaster in my part of the world partly due to the availability of our treatment, but mostly due to the nature of our snakes.

I have always liked reptiles and amphibians and have kept and studied them as far back as I can remember. In fact, my earliest memory ever is of a little brown snake coiled beneath the grass clump I pulled away from the edge of the driveway. I was two and the snake was most likely a De Kay's brown snake (in retrospect, of course).

One of the biggest regrets in my career was the fact that I missed the spectacle of the guy who showed up in the waiting room with the huge head of a boa constrictor attached to his upper arm. The rest of the snake had been removed, I suppose for transport reasons or to end the cross-species misunderstanding.

Most of the snake tales from the ED concern reptiles that are too small to eat us. The presence of venom is the issue. Most of our venomous bites swell and hurt and get antivenin and get admitted, with only a little drama. It's more fun when they bring the snake:

The man was distraught. "The snake bit me and now I can't move my arm." He indicated several little holes on his hand. He then demonstrated trying to lift his arm. He was unsuccessful.

A bucket on the floor caught my attention.

"This the snake, I guess?" I hoped I didn't sound too sympathetic. I was a little saddened to see the dead snake.

I was a paying member of the National Herpetological Society in fourth grade, so it took me no time to recognize the snake as a nonvenomous water snake. I have had several for pets (easy to feed, but feisty).

"This is the snake that bit you? You're certain?" I asked.

My identification of red-bellied watersnake did not convince him that it was not venomous. I gave a brief little lecture, pointing out the non-concerning bite marks and the lack of swelling on himself. I pointed out several identifying features on the snake. He was not convinced and still trying to move his arm, which was dangling by his side.

I then held the snake in front of him and inserted my ungloved finger in the snake's mouth in a manner that demonstrated my confidence that there were no venomous teeth in there. I was a little careful I would not get tooth pricks myself. This was the antidote and he began moving his arm. Cured.

Snakes are not the only venomous creatures around.

This patient showed up in severe pain. He came by ambulance. The source of his agony was a peculiar lesion on his forearm. It was about four centimeters by two centimeters, bright red, slightly raised and patterned. Several small angry bumps were evenly spaced in symmetrical rows.

He said he felt intense pain when he was working on cutting up an oak tree. He then showed me what he held in a cup. It was a tan hairball coughed up by a cat. Of course, that's not really what it was, but that's exactly what it looked like. It was four centimeters long. I did not touch it, surmising that the regular pattern of the painful lesion fit my idea of a caterpillar sting.

A little Dr. Googling later and I had a precise diagnosis: Tree Asp sting. I have since seen one other case, and the second patient was also experiencing severe pain and acting like a burn victim. More pain than a snakebite, but less than a femur fracture.

The Tree Asp guy would have probably said his pain was a "Ten!" on the scale from one to ten, but this would not have been true. Maybe an eight. The pain scale does not lead you towards truth.

I have always had run-ins with this pain scale. I have no doubt that a smart student could show me a well-designed study that proves this scale's validity, but you should never underestimate the ability of scientists to obscure reality. They somehow can design studies to weed out all the factors that will actually occur in real life, which is what occurs the vast majority of the time.

I always thank people for giving themselves reasonable pain scores, because the majority of these responses are not helpful.

"It's a twenty!" yells the patient. "I'm a twenty!"

I will give the researchers some credit. It is definitely therapeutic for me to hear triage nurses respond to such abominations (that is a cool word, abomination, it's what Mussolini said as he went off to war. That is a bad joke. A better and stolen one in the same genre is: "What do you call a cow that swallowed dynamite? Abominable. Hahaha! A bomb in a bull?")

This pain scale listed right beside the temperature as a vital sign is also negotiable.

"It's a ten!" says any of a number of back-pains, arthritic knees, or sore throat patients eating chips. When I hear such a travesty, I'll instruct the scribe, in the patient's hearing, "Do not write that down."

"I'll give you a two," I bargain.

After a disoriented pause, I typically get something like, "It's at least a nine." The patient will look up from his cell phone.

Having read books about bargaining, I maintain eye contact and offer:

"I'll give you a four, tops."

The patient counteroffers, "Eight."

"OK, scribe. Write down five for his pain." Of course, now I have to work a little harder to keep this patient happy.

In the ER setting, I honestly doubt that the pain scale has ever helped me help anyone. It may help my chart show improvement, but avoiding numbers, and just using words like "better" to document pain response, would save a lot of wear and tear on triage nurses' nerves. I do not doubt that it is useful in some settings, but the scale is not of much use for me in an ED setting.

To prove my point, the pain scale just distracted me from the story about the Tree Asp. I advise you to google an image of it. They look a little more like a living creature in the photographs than the disheveled specimen my patient brought in, but they are still a little unreal.

I guess we can count dead animals in this chapter. I saw this guy that was almost killed by a pack of dead rats. He was a homeless gentleman who staggered and limped into the ED.

Some of the homeless seem to handle their hard conditions fairly well. They are cheerful and don't appear too unhealthy. They can manage to jump the hurdles surrounding them regarding shelter rules, finding good clothes, and keeping clean. One guy managed to save thousands of donated dollars crumpled and stashed on his person.

This man was not one of those homeless. He appeared too beaten down, too mentally fragile, too pitiful to handle anything. He could not talk clearly, but he made it obvious that he was in significant pain and that something significant was wrong with his posterior. The landmarks through his trousers were vague, but he seemed to be pointing to his rectum.

Upon appropriately undressing him, I began my approach. Not trusting exam gloves much (I found a mosquito baked in one once), I wore two. He got in position and, seeing nothing to cause pain externally, I began the Internal Probe.

I immediately hit something sharp. With rapidity enhanced by fear, I withdrew my finger and inspected it. There was no hole in the glove. There was no blood spot under the glove. There were no persistent symptoms of pain in my finger. That was close. The area was not likely to produce a clean wound.

Sadly, my first suspicion was that someone had broken off a broomstick or something similar in him. I say "sadly," because there are definitely evil people around who do things to the defenseless. Further inspection (with tools) revealed a firmly wedged object with sharp protrusions.

The surgeon I consulted stopped by a week later just to reveal his findings to me (I like these guys).

"Rat bones."

"What? did he place a rat in . . ." he didn't give me time to finish, and I was OK with that.

"No, it was a bunch of rat bones from more than one rat, clumped together. I am almost sure he had eaten them. I guess it might not have been a rat, but it was a number of some small rodents," he said.

For some reason, my wife was really struck by this episode. Cows and rats are both mammals. So, in my book, as long as the guy cleanly butchered and cooked the latter, and he was not a vegetarian, I don't count his eating of rats, per se, as a horror. I would count the bones, the homelessness, and his piteous inability to benefit from the numerous excellent local food pantries and shelters—I would count those as a horror. I guess that's what really bothered my wife.

In this animal chapter, I will include fish. There was an impressive lady (cleaned her own fish) who had stuck a two-inch catfish spine into the front of her thigh.[36] The family had removed the rest of the fish and helpfully left me a little nubbin of spine to grasp. Expecting a fight, I numbed her up well. I underestimated my opponent.

The spine's little barbs held her skin so well, that I could lift her leg off the bed with the hemostat clamped on the spine. I had to use a scalpel to cut down the barbed side of the spine before I could pull it out.

That reminds me of the fish spine I removed from a local man's finger. It was actually completely under the skin, no

---

[36] This was an accident. Amazingly, that will not be obvious to any seasoned practitioners. People do odd things to themselves.

nubbin to grab, and right near a joint. I used a portable fluoroscope to visualize and remove this sucker, then irrigated the wound well. Because the foreign body was completely under the skin and near a joint, I was performing somewhat above my pay grade and significantly decreased this guy's risk of serious finger problems. I saved him at least a thousand dollars to boot. My share of his bill was realistically about thirty dollars, since I get paid by the hour. My company charged him around $600 total (admittedly not cheap—just better than the alternatives).

I was annoyed a few months later to see an article in our local paper discussing this very fish spine. The guy, who recovered fully, was complaining about the extreme cost of such a simple procedure. Ha! I just made it look easy. It is no simple thing to get a foreign body that is hidden under the skin, especially a small, flesh-colored one. You can't win, even when you think you did.

Speaking of not winning, listen to this:

One of our pediatricians staggered up to the counter. He said he was having an allergic reaction (it may have been a bee sting?). My first guess was that he was right. He did not actually pass out until I had half-carried him a good ways to an open room. His vital signs were consistent with anaphylactic shock.

I ordered some epinephrine, steroids, fluids, and Benadryl and left the room as the nurses got the IV access.

I went to the nursing station and grabbed the resident who was rotating with us and said, "Drop everything else and just take care of Dr. L—. We'll admit him to the unit when we get him stabilized." There was exactly zero delay in his care, things went as smoothly as possible, he rapidly improved, and was wheeled on upstairs. Yay, a win!

Not so fast. Too soon to celebrate.

A month or so later, this same pediatrician was rounding in the ED with his residents. I think he wanted the ED staff to hear as he said loudly, "The ED almost killed me last month. They just left me in some room and a resident came and saved me."

My normal passive-aggressive approach was substituted for a more assertive one as I pounced. I don't mind that he was too much in shock to remember me personally (when someone knows your name, it's usually for a complaint), but I did mind the false accusation against the ED doctors and staff in general.

Spider!

"Spider bites" are an extremely common occurrence in the ED. The quotes are to let you know that they are almost never truly spider bites. "Abscess" does not have the same cachet, and so is typically resisted as the obvious explanation for the problem. People believe they have been bitten by these invisible spiders in the coldest of winter or dozens of times at once. There are enough real spider stories around to keep the more common imaginary spiders alive.

The night before writing the above paragraph, I had a patient who presented with "Brown Recluse Bite." This patient, having witnessed no spider and felt no bite (unfortunately this is common in real spider bites), assumed that of the two dozen smaller scabs surrounded by pink that were scattered about his arms and shoulders, only one big one was a spider bite. There was no difference in appearance from the others, other than it was slightly bigger and little more tender.

"I doubt it is a spider bite, it just looks like all these other places scattered all over. The pattern makes it look like you do a lot of skin picking," I said.

His rebuttal was, "I *know* those aren't spider bites, but this big one is."

"Don't worry, I'm going to treat you the exact same way as if I did think it was a spider bite," was my final answer. You have to pick your battles.

In a similar vein, make sure your treatment addresses whatever the patient has diagnosed themselves with if at all possible. Sometimes their self-diagnosis is so far-fetched it is easy to disabuse them of it. However, some people are very difficult to convince, and bugs tend to additionally impair mentation.

Even bugs that are not there can cause problems. Numerous times in my career, I have run across an interesting malady with an interesting name: "Delusions of parasitosis." There are also more tedious names for this phenomenon wherein the individual believes themselves to be infested with some type of bug or worm. They will point to freckles, show you the roots of hair they have pulled out, or cell phone videos which, like UFO videos, never quite get to the truth out there.

For these patients, their visit with you, as well as the multiple other doctor visits they have had, will likely be frustrating, for these are very difficult cases. It is nearly impossible to reassure these people that the infestation is not in their skin. These people are often normal in every other way. The delusion is fixed and narrowly limited.

I strongly advise you to consult Dr. Google to get the latest real information and treatment plan for this disease.

Also, bugs that really were there sometimes do not cause problems:

"The computer said, 'Bee sting,' is that what's up?" I asked the normal-looking patient.

"Yessir, I was stung by a bee." The man was perfectly comfortable, sitting on the bed. I waited for any additional plot reveals. Nothing.

"When did you get stung?" I probed.

"A couple of days ago," he added nonchalantly.

"Are you allergic to bees?" This may be it.

"No."

"Where did you get stung?" Still looking for answers.

The guy looked down at his left forearm intently, then his right, then he bobbled back and forth between his normal forearms a few times.

"I can't remember," he shrugged.

"OK, well, I'll get you out of here shortly," I said cheerily.

"Ok, thanks, Doc," was his also cheery and seemingly genuine response.

I have no idea. Usually when the complaint seems inexplicably minor, there is a girlfriend or boyfriend down the hall with a more substantial complaint.

Some decide to lecture folks on inappropriate visits, and hospitals periodically go on purges to try to improve the quality of patients. I just try to treat them with dignity and move along. Of course, "dignity" can involve teasing them about coming in for something lame, but there is no need for anyone to take offense. There will always be differences in risk tolerance, intelligence, and common sense.

I think it is better for all just to quit trying to figure people out. I go ahead and assume that everyone is a drug seeker in the ED at three a.m. for no good reason. Then I give up on judging and treat them all.

"Why are they here at three a.m. for this?" the young student asks.

"Why not?" the old master replies.

Expectations just get in the way of objectivity and can affect your clinical judgement right at the most critical juncture.

I was trying to remember more bug stories, but instead remembered a non-bug story. This isn't even an animal story and starts a new category: foreign objects.

Rings and Things

I saw the teenager with the facial piercing glowing a bright chartreuse in room 3A. The piercing was on his nose and impossible to not notice. He was sitting up in bed, and I glanced his way several times as I walked around. I was not shocked by this, but I was prodded into thought about all these increasingly dramatic piercings, and how enough is enough.

When he finally rose to "next" on the list, I found the piercing was unintentional—it was a fishing lure. I felt the need to recalibrate my sense of normal. Next patient:

"Can I try it?" The PA was enthusiastic. He didn't really need my permission, but being a nice fellow, he didn't want me to have to sign off later on a disgruntled patient's chart. What he wanted to try was a new trick he read about for removing fishhooks.

It involved pressing firmly on the shaft to unload the barb, then yanking on a loop of string wrapped through the curve of the hook. The hook pops right out! Quick, clean, simple. No need for numbing meds or cutting. I'm sure it has worked well many times. Still . . .

"Sure, but you'll look like an idiot if it doesn't come out when you yank," was my professional opinion. He returned a few moments later.

"I looked like an idiot."

The rent is high when you live on the cutting edge.

It is pretty common to run across things that aren't where they should be. My half-joke of "Is it childproof?" proved to be important when I was unable to take off the top of the pill bottle nestled in the man's rectum. It would have been easy to grasp with the top removed, but now it eluded all my tools' grasp, and I had to pass him off to the surgeon, who opted for the slow game and let the man pass it himself with the aid of laxatives.

Earrings, nose rings, tongue piercings, nipple rings, belly button rings—a veritable bell choir of adornments that I have removed after infection sets in, or they get sucked out of sight beneath the skin.

Rings get stuck on swollen fingers. A guy had a tungsten ring stuck on his. Armed with knowledge from a recent consult (Dr. Google, in association with Dr. YouTube), I approached the finger with Vise-grips obtained from maintenance.

The theory was that applying intense pressure to the ring would shatter it, without any bending. Not wanting to shatter the finger, I was incrementally increasing the forces I brought to bear on the ring.

The owner of the finger and ring grew impatient with my cautious approach. He took the Vise-grips from me and, straining, burst the ring he once owned into tungsten shards pinging off the floor. I guess he still owned it, but it was in numerous pieces.

Another story from the wee hours. A different guy had made himself a nice ring from a sturdy stainless-steel nut. He did not seem proud of his foray into the world of hand-made jewelry because this heirloom-to-be was inflicting significant pain to the finger held in its embrace.

Stuck rings are truly an emergency, and it is possible to lose a finger. We were not fooling around when we tried our specially designed ring cutters, manual and electric. These merely shined the unnecessarily thick ring. (A matter of taste; I suppose his aesthetics may have favored thick.)

Maintenance brought me all their hand tools. Wire cutters, side cutters, hacksaw—all these did not work for one reason or another.

"I wish I had my Dremel tool," the resident with me heard me say.

"I can go get mine at home, ten minutes from here!" He was gung ho.

I thought I might as well get that option in motion while I looked for others, so I sent him off. He returned with the tool, a complete kit with the nice cutoff disks. I started planning my approach, gaining the feel and heft of the tool.

"Can I do it?" he asked. I looked over the young resident. He did not appear to be the real handyman type, but he was certainly eager. It was his tool. He drove all the way home for it. I wore myself down.

"Sure," I said, hoping any misgivings were hidden.

I was nervous throughout the procedure. It is hard to supervise someone else doing something that you would be nervous doing yourself. There was a 30,000-rpm abrasive disk trying to slip and cut the patient's finger off. There were sparks lighting the room that were not as celebratory in this setting as they might be on the Fourth of July. The sudden shower of them made the patient jump, but not me. I was ready for worse.

The patient noticed the growing heat just as I began spraying the whole operation with cooling water, making it even harder for me to maintain my grip. We could not spread the strong ring with the one cut, so we continued our demolition.

We succeeded in removing the extraordinarily sturdy ring. I think that is when my hair first started going grey.

Towards the end of my career, as a respected elder of medicine (with mostly grey hair), one of my younger bosses (a physician) came to me with a ring stuck on her finger. This was a very nice ring, of conventional precious metal, but with a nonconventional girth. It had defeated all her removal attempts, using the standard tools.

We walked together to maintenance so I could show off my broad skillset with various nonmedical devices. She was not impressed because neither was the ring. The ring sneered at the unimpressively ineffective tools. Dr. Patient and I both noticed our "This could be a real problem" silent alarms sounding.

While making gruelingly slow progress, a helpful nurse showed up. He offered his expensive folding trauma shears and pointed out:

"Look, it has a ring cutter." None of the others around had noticed that particular feature on these pricey scissors.

This device cut through the ring pretty easily. It did require some force, and multiple cuts were still required due to the sturdiness of the heirloom. (I said it was a nice ring.)

I was happy when we finally pried the remaining ring off the swollen finger. My boss was also happy, but her mood changed quickly with an "ouch" as she noticed the cut I had made on her hand. I was shocked because I thought I was practicing careful muzzle control on the scissors, but clearly, I was not.

The boss and I were impressed. We both sprung the money for a pair of those shears. She healed up well from the little cut, but I was not scheduled on her side of the department after that. (Note for boss: I am chalking that up to a coincidence?).

8

Air

Do not underestimate the power of invisible things. Covid-19 and radiation may quickly spring to mind, but air should be right up there in the top of any such list, as its absence quickly alerts you to its importance.

This determined-looking young lady was sitting up in bed. She was not going to open her mouth despite the presence of numerous persons interested in her doing so. (This is not the patient whose mouth I set on fire.)

The police officers surrounding her bed were trying hard to get her to open her mouth because they were interested in examining the contents of a small bag she allegedly was sequestering there.

Pessimists that they are, the police were suspecting drugs. No amount of coaxing or warning or legal threats from Team Police, now aided by the also pessimistic medical side, was successful. Since we were not sure of the safety of the bag's contents, nor the bag's integrity, Team Medical placed her in an observation room on a pulse oximeter and cardiac monitor.

This proved helpful, as the doctor (myself) directly observed a change in the patient's facial expression. I saw her determination morph to concern to alarm to horror to that eyes-rolling-to-the-back-of-your-head-meme as the girl began asphyxiating on the alleged bag and fell backwards against the bed, beginning to lose alleged consciousness.

So, we didn't need the monitors after all, since I saw the immediate deterioration. I was like a human pulse ox. So, sounding my alarm, I rushed in the room and others joined me.

Team Medical pried open the now loose jaws and retrieved a small bag of white powder. "Baking soda?" The police didn't appreciate my joke.

The airway was grateful of my help, however, and the ineffectual inhalations became less so as the patient soon caught her breath.

This patient's case was rewarding, but in general I do not like deteriorating patients. It is sometimes OK if I know the reason, it is expected, and everyone is at peace with a slow, non-suffering demise. If the patient is going downhill, especially if you're not sure why, then multiple, frequent visits are essential. This lets family know that you are concerned or even worried about the patient. This helps prepare them for a bad outcome. You do not want them to think that you were caught off guard or not taking their loved one seriously enough.

Unfortunately, nothing about this next guy's situation was peaceful. He was clearly worsening, and the family was distraught and demanding answers.

I was doing the above things right, but this family was tough and criticizing the hospital, nurses, and me unfairly. I strove to make sure the family mood was "correct" for the patient's level of seriousness, and I did what I could to make sure they were aware that I was trying hard and doing everything reasonable. Despite my efforts, his ailment was winning. I ended up deciding it was a tricky case of sepsis, without the usual clues of fever, low blood pressure, or other signs of infection. But I was treating and checking all the usual suspects and informing the family throughout this time.

As he continued to deteriorate over a few hours (slowly by ED standards), he quickened his pace on his climb up the stairway to heaven and now needed to be intubated.

An unpleasant surprise popped up when I discovered that all of the laryngoscope blade bulbs were out or missing, and there were no others nearby. We called for upstairs backup, but that would take dangerously long.

I suddenly and unprecedentedly decided to improvise and use a penlight held on top of a wooden tongue blade. This actually went pretty well, and the intubation was smooth and quick.

I doubt the patient ultimately did well, but I was not unhappy with my care of the patient and proud of the jury-rigged intubation. I felt it was unjust that I could not mention my exceptional intubation innovation to the family (then they would attack me and the hospital for the laryngoscope logistics fiasco). I have never had to intubate that way again.

Even when all the tools are at hand, I still have had numerous cases involving difficult airways. The technology has improved over the years. In residency, we did blind nasotracheal intubations; when I started in the ED, we used laryngoscopes. Now we have several fiberoptic video choices. Most of the cases in this book occurred prior to fiberoptics in our department.

I treated a middle-aged man who had drunk some lye in a suicide attempt. The caustic, melt-your-eyes-out drain cleaner stuff. I was aware of the danger of this stuff for more than one reason: labels on bottles, medical school, and common sense. I was also particularly aware of the airway danger, because a man had died in our ED a month prior from the same ingestion; intubation had been impossible.

"Are you OK?" I asked the calm-looking man seated in 2A.

"Yes," was the normal-sounding reply. I wasn't expecting normal.

A few more questions and a quick exam, then, "Are you hoarse at all?" I asked, deciding he may know his own voice better than me.

"Yeah, I may be a little hoarse." It was not noticeable to me, but it was all the excuse I needed.

"Intubating in 2A!" Soon a small swarm helped with all the setup necessary. Our meds kicked in and the patient drifted off to sleep, muscles relaxed.

When I got my laryngoscope blade into position, I was frightened to discover that I could not see the landmarks I needed to intubate him. Despite his normal-to-a-stranger-sounding voice, his vocal cords were completely obscured by huge bulges of swollen tissue erupting from all directions in the back of his throat.

However, disaster was dealt the losing hand when the tube slid in place without my being able to see anything. *Medical Pearl: Doing your own cricoid pressure or moving the larynx for yourself will sometimes give you an aimpoint.*

Esophageal Rupture

I had a similar fright in this dramatic case, illustrating numerous issues:

The physician assistant alerted me to the patient who had severe chest pain after coughing unusually hard. We both were thinking: esophageal rupture.

I was proud of myself for spotting the tiny line of air in the wrong place, confirming the diagnosis. So far so good; things were going fast. I knew this disorder needed to be treated quickly. I paged the chest surgeon.

"Right, go ahead and get a chest CT to check it out," I was told. OK, the chest surgeon was on the case. But not exactly like I'd hoped.

I phoned him around an hour later. "The CT's back and is consistent with a rupture."

The answer was, "Well, I won't be able to take care of it because I'll be out of town tomorrow. You'll have to transfer him."

What?

This annoyed me because without his presumed availability, I would have called for a transfer without waiting for a CT.

These injuries are time-sensitive, and the receiving hospital might have rather done their own CT.

Two or three phone calls later got me this from a chest surgeon at the Big City hospital: "I can't accept the patient since you have a thoracic surgeon at your facility." My "But, buts" were ineffective, so I resigned myself to recall the thoracic surgeon I spoke with earlier.

"I will be gone tomorrow; I can't do it." Our local guy was still unbudgeable.

Getting desperate, I requested something unusual: "Just please tell me clearly that you are refusing the patient."

"Sure," he said. "I refuse the patient."

Armed with this refusal, I renegotiated with the specialist surgeons in the Big City, and they accepted the man. Yay! Wait, too soon to celebrate.

Of course, the clock had not been paused for any of these delays of game. At this point, the man began to deteriorate. It had been around three hours since his presentation. His breathing was getting harder. All those esophageal contaminants and air loose in the mediastinum were wreaking havoc.

The faint line of air we saw on his chest x-ray had blown up into the rice-crispy crackle feel of crepitance all about his neck. All of this subcutaneous air just got worse. His neck began to really swell.

A long transport was looking too scary for this patient without a protected airway. He was moving lots of air, just not into the right place.

By the time we were ready for the intubation, he had blown up like a toad. He was not quite as inflated as the girl who was killed in the car wreck, with her damaged trachea or bronchus, but his neck was much larger than usual.

My brain knew that intubation was essential for this man, and that the leaked air might make things difficult, but my nerves were not quite prepared for the actual sight of it. His insides were bulging *in* as much as his outsides were bulging *out.* The lining of his throat puffed out inward, filling his throat, until there was not much left to see; I had no chance of seeing the cords.

The intubation (largely by feel) was immediately successful, and we did not have to call in the big guns from upstairs. *Medical Pearl: It's better to be lucky than smart.*

The big guns are the anesthesiology team. We occasionally call them for not-so-urgent intubations that are likely to be difficult. We also call them for intubations we cannot get.

Sometimes they get the intubation so easily it makes us look like idiots and the nurses unceremoniously change their own status from "high alert" to "no big deal" when anesthesia arrives and succeeds. In one case, anesthesia was not what was needed. We needed the really big guns—a surgeon—but there was no time.

Cricothyrotomy

The older man was clearly struggling to breathe. He was gasping for air and barely conscious. Since the techniques and drugs have dramatically improved the success rate of ED intubation over the decades, this procedure gets my full attention, but doesn't frighten me. Well, unless there are obvious problems, like a fist-sized tongue. (Angioedema. Anesthesia was unavailable, another lucky intubation with cords never visualized.) But there were no obvious problems with this guy.

Our setup and the start of the intubation was routine (in ED terms) until I got to the part where I'm supposed to see the vocal cords, my landmark to insert the tube. I was stopped cold. I was lost. I could not understand the anatomy. Parts were not exactly recognizable to me, and I knew something wasn't right. I blinked and self-assessed; readjusted my reading glasses. I didn't seem to be the problem.

A little suction and probing around didn't work. All I saw was blood and *something*. Maybe a mass? I have always said that quitting is underrated, so here was my chance to demonstrate the power of quitting.

So I quit. "Call anesthesia!" We began bagging the guy, thankfully easy in his case and aided by the medication we had given him. I asked the nurses to get the cricothyrotomy[37] kit just in case, and I looked at its contents through the clear package.

This was one of those blissful days when anesthesia seemed to be waiting around the corner.

I greeted him with, "I'm happy to see you! I don't have a clue; I think there's some mass. I never saw cords or even the epiglottis." The anesthesiologist came with some of his own tools.

He looked inside the man briefly and said, "I see what you mean. I can't tube this guy either."

I had prepared myself for this. "Well, I guess I'll crike[38] him." I may have sounded nonchalant, or I may have sounded nervous, overly nonchalant. However I sounded, I was definitely non-nonchalant. This was a high-risk situation.

I felt a little pressure to keep my cool in front of the young anesthesiologist. We ED doctors have an inferiority complex regarding this specialty. But mostly I was just in my "never panic" mode.

---

[37] Poking a hole in the airway just below the cords to get in a tube, one of the most common life-saving procedures faked by movie stars.

[38] Shorthand for the cricothyrotomy. Most medical persons are amused by the stilted talk of the medical world in Hollywood. We are almost always less "professional" in our speech, but more professional in our actions than our fake peers.

I opened the package I'd been studying (It had been two decades since the last time I opened one.) Here we go. It's like deciding to jump off the high dive. Leaving the board, suspended in the air—that's when you make the cut.

Or stab the needle in the guy's trachea, which is how I actually started this one. Once you get the needle in and get air in the syringe, you thread a wire inside the trachea. This Seldinger idea is great for getting lots of types of tubes in people. The man now had a wire protruding from his trachea and out into the trauma room.

I made a small vertical cut below his Adam's apple on both sides of the wire sticking vertically from the neck. Thankfully, he had an Adam's apple; lots of padding in this area can make knowing where you are impossible. (I was fully aware of a death a few weeks back when a colleague's cricothyrotomy was impossible.)

Not a lot of blood. That's good. I threaded the assembled tracheostomy tube on the wire and shoved the tip of the dilator in. It stopped before I thought it should. That's not good.

It appeared that my guide wire turned north, when it should have turned south. Minor setback—I'd just reach back in time and use the old-fashioned, open approach. I kept the wire in for some guidance. Old meets new. It was pretty easy to cut and dissect down the wire and cut an opening in the trachea, at the cricothyroid membrane.

I relaxed for one second until it became apparent that the connector to the ventilating bag wasn't present or was wrong or something. While awaiting another trach tube, I was about to ask for a regular endotracheal tube. One of my colleagues had done this in the numerous cricothyrotomies he performed over the years. (How did he get all those cases? Maybe I try harder to intubate?)

The anesthesiologist stole my line. "Just put in an ET tube," he said.

Shoot. I was going to say that. Just missed my chance. I could feel my cool factor slipping away, and I could sense the very capable charge nurse judging me while she was making other important things happen in the room.

I now removed the wire from the hole in the neck. This was a jump from the low diving board. The blood was not a problem, I enlarged the hole in the cricothyroid membrane, and I easily fed the tube down the hole on the correct course to the south.

I was truly beginning to relax as we bagged him through his new "Definitive Airway." We secured it to the neck with a regular ET tube holder. (This worked great and was my idea.)

"You can cut it off above the balloon," said the helpful young know-it-all.

I knew that and had already been headed that direction. This anesthesiologist was quick on the draw and had shot me down twice.

There was one last micro-humiliation to come: I was readying the scissors to cut the tube shorter and had located my level above the spot where the little balloon tube enters the side.

I first aligned the scissors along either side of the tube, low and close to the neck because it was a somewhat moving target. I was working my way up to the intended length, when:

"No! Higher, above the balloon!" he got in his final shot.

I knew that also. I wasn't going to cut in the wrong place and deflate the balloon. I was hoping that he did not kill the last germ of respect for me the lofty charge nurse may have been infected with.

The code in 2A was a large man. He had been eating at a restaurant and suddenly collapsed. Choking was suspected, and

Heimlich maneuvers had been attempted without improvement. EMS was bagging him on arrival and had just started CPR.

On using the laryngoscope to look inside his airway for the intubation, I noticed the most likely culprit. "Magill forceps!" I said in my best surgeon imitation.

Using the long, curved tool, I pulled out a ten-inch-long strip of steak, medium rare. I was hoping this maneuver would help resolve the cardiac arrest. CPR was ongoing.

I returned the laryngoscope to position with the tube in hand—but wait, I saw more. I pulled out another ten-inch strip of gristly steak.

I do not know how this man faired in the long run. It could have gone either way. He had a short trip in, but the bagging couldn't have been very effective in getting oxygen to his brain.

As in the lye ingestion case above, many of our intubations are to protect the airways of patients who may be breathing well enough, for now. But if we know trouble is ahead, we can't hesitate too long.

In burn victims, evidence of the inhalation of hot fumes or smoke includes singed hair or soot in the sputum (carbonaceous sputum sounds better). Both of these patients had such signs.

I was the only doctor on duty that morning. Two housefire victims came in simultaneously. One was reported to be a fifty-year-old woman, the other nineteen. They were both badly burned all over. At first glance, seventy-five percent of their skin surface, plus. They were still very alive and breathing on their own, but it was obvious what needed to be done.

The help that came from upstairs was a nurse anesthetist. The patients were in adjacent beds in the same room. "So many milligrams of a certain drug!" I called. That wasn't exactly my words, I just can't remember what we used. For clarity and efficiency in this situation, I just called out orders for medications for both patients.

"A hundred of Succ!"[39] I remember that drug. The anesthetist intubated one patient while I intubated the other in stereo.

We transferred both patients to burn centers. Beds were short in these places on that day, so one went to one Big City and the other patient went to another Big City.

I got a call a few weeks later giving me an update. (These burn centers are amazing.) I was told, "You gave us the wrong patient!" At some point, someone guessed wrong about which patient was fifty and which was nineteen. They were burned really badly. It would have been an easy mistake, and I might have made it (but I doubt it).

I do not recall hearing about the older lady (I am almost sure she died), but the younger one made our paper as "Girl Survives 90% Burns."

There are also times we make perfectly good airways into problems by giving certain medications.

"You've got to intubate him!" This wasn't the first time the student said this. My annoyance grew as his urgings seemed more and more reasonable the longer this person wasn't breathing.

We had sedated this patient with an ultrashort-acting barbiturate, Brevital. I really liked this drug because it had made the care of shoulder dislocations and the performance of painful procedures much easier. It made things easier on you and the patient and was a great improvement regarding safety as well as suffering.

I first learned about it from a Tulane orthopedic resident. She was the rare female orthopedist at the time, and they are still fairly rare, as ortho is still a mostly male domain. (I blame the sports emphasis and physical nature of repairing bones.)

---

[39] Succinylcholine, as Dr. Hollywood would say. This wonder drug paralyzes all the muscles but your heart.

At the time, I happened to be on the Pharmacy and Therapeutics Committee, where all the really smart people who knew how to do math gathered; the PharmDs. They once were smart enough to avoid working at night, but they seem to have lost this ability lately. Anyway, the pharmacy committee was convinced, and we were allowed to use the medication in the ED.

One thing I did not like about the drug was what it could do to patients like the one I was just discussing. The student urged me to intubate the patient because the Brevital had caused laryngospasm and prevented him from making even the slightest inhalation.

The overexcitable student and my own pessimism finally won the debate. I was already prepared and used the laryngoscope blade to see my target.

I saw something I don't usually see. The vocal cords were snapped shut. Just as I was about to push a tube between the cords (I hoped I could), they popped apart in front of me, his airway opened, and he took a deep breath. I maintained my position and watched his cords let in a few more breaths before I slid the laryngoscope back out.

Optimism wins again! Although pessimism wins more often. Actually, "You can't win" wins most often.

Assorted Cases

Case 1

This was a scary intubation. Her mouth looked small, and she had never uttered a word in her twenty years of life. I don't recall the congenital condition she had. The family said she sometimes made high-pitched noises and that was it. I chose a number-five tube as my best educated guess, and the intubation went well.

Someone in the ICU was raising a big fuss about the too-small tube, and they consulted anesthesia for a bigger one. After hearing the story about the patient never talking, he refused to change it out because he was also afraid her anatomy would be tricky. This increased my street cred with the ICU.

Case 2

This older man kept getting choked. Something was blocking his tracheostomy tube. It was a round, hard marble of dried mucus. It would intermittently get stuck in his airway like a ball valve, then fall away from the opening and rattle away in his trachea. It was very tricky to remove and required the patient to coordinate his exhalation with my retrieval. I didn't want him to suck any of the fragments into his lungs.

9
Hearts

You can have more air than you need, but you will still not live long without your heart or some other pump moving blood around. Some of the most dramatic times in the ED involves hearts. Most of the successful codes involve malfunctioning hearts as the primary cause, because CPR is unlikely to work if there's much else wrong with a patient.

Back from the Dead

The young man with bright blond, curly hair had collapsed while doing some volunteer work. I noticed the hair was the same color and texture of the girl who got mauled by the dogs. Bystanders had begun CPR immediately, and this was continued by EMS who also began ACLS care on the trip in.

He was still coding on arrival and getting CPR. I believe he was already intubated; if not, I did it quickly once we got him. We continued CPR, repeated doses of epinephrine, defibrillated him, repeated epi, added more drugs, and defibrillated him several more times. We got occasional effective rhythms with a pulse, but these were very brief episodes.

We kept this up until we had exhausted one or two of the protocols. Some of the nurses began sending signals that enough was enough. No one wants to get a heartbeat back if the brain is gone. The nurses were right to raise the issue. I defended my persistence by pointing out his significant periods of time with a pulse, his youth, and how these factors would decrease his chances of brain damage if we "got him back." I certainly would have already stopped if his brain had been very old or contained within an ill or infirm body.

Finally, after almost an hour, he regained a pulse that didn't immediately evaporate. We kept some drips going and he made further gains and we were able to measure a blood pressure. He stabilized and I went to talk to Mom.

I started off as usual, but veered into unusual territory: "Well, he is as sick as you can possibly be. He has been basically dead off and on for most of the past hour and a half, but he has had good CPR, and when he does come back, his color returns, and he looks good. You need to be prepared for at least three outcomes. He may not survive the night, this is probably the most likely outcome, *but* . . . I will not be surprised at all if he survives because he is young, healthy, and had periods of time with a pulse.

"Secondly, he may survive but have any number of problems, including not waking up.

"I kind of hesitate to give you the third scenario, because it is the least common, but it is possible he will fully recover. I don't often mention this possibility because it is so rare, but he had consistent, good CPR, and he is young and fit. He may survive with no problems at all. I will not be shocked by any of these three outcomes."

The mother seemed to understand and have the appropriate amount of concern and hope. I wasn't so sure about giving her the third possibility of full recovery and thought it might backfire and worsen any bad news when it came.

I wasn't shocked, but I *was* pleasantly surprised when he fully recovered. He had a cardiac abnormality that produced the arrythmia. Cardiologists were able to prevent future recurrences.

This curly blond-haired young man was now paired in my mind with the curly blond dog-mauled girl. This was a very good thing for my soul.

Keep up the Pacing

C BIG K. That is the perfect mnemonic. It tells you what the problem is (high potassium, K), and it gives you the treatment, all in a reasonable order: calcium, bicarb, insulin, glucose, and kayexalate. The treatment outlined by this mnemonic is frequently lifesaving. It prevented my patient with the potassium of >12 from ever getting anything worse than an abnormal EKG (widened QRS complex)! *Note: Twelve was as high as our lab measured!*[40]

Newly presenting renal failure is very common in my area, and it is a very common cause of high potassium. It pops up frequently enough that I often treat for hyperkalemia in certain cardiac arrests even with no history of renal disease. I had two nearly identical cases with hyperkalemia. Both were older women with severe bradycardia. Their pulses were in the thirties and they were hypotensive. This situation justified external pacing: rhythmically zapping their hearts using pads placed on the chest.

I had the bright idea to use the ultrasound machine to verify that the external pacer was capturing, and I used this technique on both patients. Actually seeing the heart pump faster assured me of capture immediately, allowing me to use the least amount of electricity that was effective (seventy milliamps for

---

[40] Sorry. Too many things in this paragraph for a footnote. Just keep moving, you're are not missing much.

both). Both patients tolerated this repeated shock well, and I had no need to deeply sedate them.

On the first patient, after getting a good radial pulse at a paced rate of seventy, I paged the cardiologist for help. "It's probably her electrolytes, just treat those," he said and hung up. I was a little upset at this inadequate amount of assistance, as this was a pretty scary patient for me. In half an hour (years, it felt), the labs came back with a very high potassium.

Typical treatment (C BIG K) resulted in her pulse now exceeding the pacer, and I was able to turn it off. Her pressure normalized. The medicine service and nephrologist took over and all was good. I left the pacer pads on the patient, just in case.

The second patient preceded precisely as before until I contacted the cardiologist.

"Don't pace her, it is too uncomfortable. I am coming," I was told.

"Uhm, I'm already pacing her, and she's tolerating it well. And she's doing better," I said.

As the cardiologist drove in, the labs returned, and the potassium was sky-high. C BIG K. Before the cardiologist arrived, the patient regained her normal rate, and I turned off pacing, leaving the pads on, of course. The cardiologist took her upstairs and put in a transvenous pacer, which never had to be turned on.

She was admitted upstairs, and all was well for me in the ED. I certainly liked the enthusiasm from this second nice cardiologist, but the first one ended up saving the patient an unnecessary procedure (in retrospect, of course, and still a reasonable precaution).

After a code goes on a while, I frequently start pulling out algorithm cards for reminders or ideas. This next case got my attention and held it for a *long* while; I used all my cards and added several more grey hairs in the process.

Iatrogenic Asystole, or I killed Him[41]

It was around two p.m., Bad Standard Time (always in effect in the ER). The fellow had a little grey in his tied-back long hair. He looked, acted, and dressed like a kindly and maturing Hell's Angel. He was sitting in 4A with his wife, and his face displayed a ready-for-what's-next look.

I was frightened when I saw that his monitor displayed ventricular tachycardia. Too fast and too wide. His blood pressure was low and on the borderline between the shock or medically-treat options for this rhythm.

Coward that I am, I paged his cardiologist to pick a side of the border.

"Oh, that guy. Yea, he's had v-tach[42] several times before. You just have to cardiovert him. Meds don't work. He takes the full two hundred joules. Shock him." The cardiologist was confident.

After making sure that I got the plan clear, I hung up and returned to the room. The patient was smiling and laughing with his wife. I did not want to kill this guy; cardioversion is no joke.

To prepare myself and make sure I was doing the right thing, I used one of my mind tricks. I re-evaluated the situation in light of an imaginary bad outcome:

"Yes, Your Honor, I know. But the rhythm was potentially lethal, his blood pressure was low, and I had clear instructions from his cardiologist who had treated him for this exact same problem before," I said in my imagination.

Now armed with my defense already prepared if the worst happened, I entered the room with resolve. The patient was a

---

[41] Iatrogenic means caused by medical care. Asystole means the heart has stopped its own electrical activity.

[42] "Ventricular tachycardia" is how Dr. Hollywood would say it, unrealistically. A life-threatening electrical malfunction.

little disappointed in the decision, but not too surprised. This was not his first ride on a bike.

The synchronizer light blipped on each monitored heartbeat as we set the defibrillator to time the shock with his own heart's electrical activity. His wife wanted to stay for moral support, having seen this before, and I let her.

The movement of his arms and noise of the *ZAP*! was followed by the ominous silence of ASYSTOLE on the monitor. His heart had completely stopped. So did everyone else's in the room, to a lesser degree.

There was lots of help, so the CPR began quickly. The team marched through the protocol with multiple shocks, meds, intubation, and more meds. Lots of CPR was done, in fact.

We coded the man for around thirty minutes, working our way all the way down to Bretylium in the old algorithm before he regained a pulse.

He had good CPR and was oxygenated well throughout, so that was good, but it sure was a long code. I was not optimistic.

After getting the stabilized, but still uber-critical man upstairs, a new colleague approached. He had been standing in the corner of the room and quietly observed me throughout the whole debacle. His helpful observation was that the whole time I was coding the man, he kept thinking, "I'm glad it's not me, I'm glad it's not me."

I also would have been glad for it not to have been me, but it was too late now. I had liked the man and felt terrible. I also knew this was potentially the big one and was worried about getting sued to oblivion.

So, what did I do? I left for the beach. However, I'm only ten percent psychopath, therefore, I didn't forget about him. I called daily to check on his status. The unit nurses informed me:

"On the vent."

"On the vent."

"Still on the vent." Then:

"Off the vent," on day four.

Maybe? I hesitated to hope. Further calls elicited descriptions of him talking, walking, and eventually gaining full recovery. That was very nice.

I saw the man a few times over the next several years, and he acted slightly miffed when I feigned fright each time I walked in his room.

I was really *feigning* feigning fright. His heart made me nervous because it had a tendency to either beat too fast or to stop. In a minute, I'll tell you a heart-too-slow story that is a little unusual.

Wait, back up. Did I say ten percent psychopath, you ask? That's right. As I mentioned in the introduction, it helps to be at least a little on the ruthless side, especially in the really hard cases where you have to do painful or invasive things to people, or if they have horrible outcomes. It is not possible to concentrate, to do your job, to save lives if you are too emotional. You cannot intubate and save the dying baby if you have tears clouding your eyes.

There are times that badly injured people with dangerous deformities are too unstable to sedate, or sometimes there's no time or no nurse available. You may have to inflict some pain to save a limb. Things can get really bloody. Grieving mothers can be pitiful sights. There are times you have to turn off your humanity if you really want to help humanity with the hard stuff.

Those things are sad truths that occur in only a small fraction of cases, but the sad adds up over the years. The following tale doesn't really illustrate what I've just been saying, but it still happened.

Poisoning

The young man collapsed in the waiting room. As we went to retrieve him, we got the story that he felt bad right after taking a shower. We were quickly getting him in the bed in 3C, when something caught my ear. Someone mentioned a spill in the garage. That's why he was taking a shower—he had spilled some liquid on himself.

"Any idea what it was?"

The negative answer was not too much of a problem, because it was soon easy to see what the substance was: an organophosphate.

The patient's pulse rate was low, his blood pressure low, and his pupils huge. I do not recall him showing the increased secretions typical of these poisonings. We placed a plastic decontamination sheet under him and washed him off on the bed. (He'd already had a shower, but . . .)

His mental status worsened over a few minutes time until he was unconscious. I was ready with the laryngoscope when he took his last inhalation. I intubated him, and the respiratory terrorist began bagging him. He may have missed two breaths.

We gave him lots and lots of atropine and some 2-pam chloride. The pharmacy was calling to ask about all the atropine we used. I think we were making a big dent in the hospital's supply. I recall his pupils actually getting smaller with the treatment; this was the opposite of the dilation you usually get with atropine. I guess the atropine was less potent than the organophosphate regarding the effects on the pupils.

We shipped him up to the ICU,[43] and he made a full recovery.

---

[43] Often thought to stand for "Intensive Care Unit." It really means "I See You,"because the gowns are open in the back. Someone else made that joke up.

I recall the real end of this guy's story, but as I write this book, it is annoying and a little troubling that I have no idea what happened to most of these patients once they left my department. The ED forces you to move along, and you are frequently moving too fast to safely look back, even to patients of the previous shift.

Missed MI

"There's a lady in 3D that needs a GI cocktail." You have to hear and respond to the diagnoses and opinions of others, but always treat these suggestions as potential red herrings, rocks to trip you up. You should also eye your own first impressions with the same skepticism.

However, in this case, I concluded that the nurse was right (as they usually are). The pain was epigastric and burning in nature. There was no sweating, difficulty breathing, radiation of the pain, or worsening of the symptoms when walking. The pain had been present for hours.

The GI cocktail relieved her pain, and I was set to send her home. My last review of the EKG showed some non-specific changes, including very slight elevations inferiorly. These ST elevations were about a line's width.

I have a very clear memory of this EKG because the woman came in the next morning with an obvious MI on the new EKG. The cardiologist read both of the EKGs at the same time and called them both positive. I thought he used the unfair advantage of hindsight. He would not have read the first EKG (mine) as an MI if he hadn't seen the second also.

I don't feel too bad about that miss because her case was atypical. I might have caught her problem if I had seen her within the last ten years, with some new tests we now have available.

Improved cardiac enzymes have made chest pain a little less tricky than in those days, but with EKGs, we are often still palm readers squinting at squiggly lines. In the case above, the lady's EKG showed what I call "lawyer changes." These are abnormalities that are not diagnostic of anything—not enough evidence to make decisions. They are, however, deadly in retrospect.

They will look definitive, magnified on an easel in the courtroom, the "non-specific changes" circled and the twelve jurors soon becoming experts in predicting the past.

Some EKGs are not equivocal at all. They are immediately spooky. Take the little two-year-old with v-tach. Please, take him. Seriously. He scared me for a couple of hours while I tried to get someone smarter than me to take over his care.

The EKG showed obvious v-tach. This is a very rare thing in a child. The child looked fine, and clearly his heart was moving around enough blood, so far. It's medically important to observe whether children are playful, but we messed up any of his plans to play; as soon as this rhythm was noted on the monitor, we did things that would make any toddler irritable: IVs, labs, defibrillator pads, x-rays. I wasn't really sure what to do next.

This was long ago and there wasn't as much specialized help around. I called three cardiologists in town, but all three of those refused to even give me a hint. "I don't take care of children," was the universal reply.

I broadened my search to the Big City. I found a very helpful guy who had me try some things. (They did not work.) He was willing to take the child if I transported him but would not take the little patient unless I intubated him prior to bundling him up to go.

The kid still looked fine. If you ignored the monitor and didn't look close enough to notice the heart pounding in his chest or feel a pulse, you would not think he was sick at all. This was just the kind of case to call anesthesiology for. Sick, but not sick enough to rush things; we could wait for the pros.

The crusty, old anesthesiologist proved to be an unexpected roadblock. His approach was not something I planned for.

"I'm not intubating that child. He's breathing fine," he said. Ouch. I had similar reservations, but the Big City pediatric cardiologist was adamant, and I trusted that he was being reasonable. Plus, he was my only option for getting the little kid cared for.

I began negotiations, recounting my difficulties finding help and singing the praises of my final rescuer and trying to persuade the anesthesiologist that this procedure was necessary to keep the transfer afloat. He was an immovable mass. I suppose these guys have to be tough, since part of their job is arguing with surgeons under very stressful circumstances.

As we were standing at the foot of the bed, mercifully (in the long run) the child had a seizure.

"OK, now I'll tube him." The anesthesiologist shrugged.

The blessed little toddler rendered my arguments trivial. He just had a seizure and convinced the man himself.

Nothing else notable happened. What caused all this in the child? This might be a board question: a tricyclic antidepressant from his grandma's purse.

I've whined about subtly abnormal EKGs, but even when EKGs are normal you can still lose.

I was suturing in the back hall when the tech slipped an EKG into my line of sight. It was perfectly normal, so normal that even the machine itself called it normal. These machines almost always overread, so "normal" is a beautiful sight to us.

"He really looks like he's having a heart attack," the tech said.

This tech had been around long enough to know, so I said, "OK, get him in the trauma room."

I was almost finished with the suturing. A couple of sutures later, I got to the trauma room a few minutes after the patient did.

He looked like he was having a heart attack to me also. Even people who are old enough to have heart attacks look young to me now, and he was no exception. He was around forty.

He was sweaty, anxious, pale. The nurses were having trouble getting leads to stick to his sweaty chest. (Note: my research indicates that nurses place these pads to ensure maximum hair loss upon removal.)

I studied the very normal EKG. It did not seem to match the patient. The squiggly lines shifted around in my brain like disseminated strongyloidiasis worms until it struck me. I had seen that EKG before.

"Hey, this is the EKG from the lady I saw earlier! This is not his." It made more sense to me now.

Somehow the tech had printed off or retrieved a prior EKG stored on the machine, or didn't print the correct one and got an old one from the bin, or who knows? Something weird happened.

It was somewhat of a relief when a new EKG showed clear ST elevations and an obvious MI. This was only a surprise to the EKG machine. Even the patient (I believe he was a nurse?) was relieved to have his suspicions confirmed.

"Code STEMI!" I yelled for dramatic effect. I did not need to yell, because the nurses were already on it and the smooth system was in motion. I remarked, "I won't get credit for remembering a normal EKG from hours ago; I'll get dinged for delaying a STEMI code for fifteen minutes."

A month later, my prognosis proved correct:

"McAnonymous!" The director stopped me in the hall. (His mother was the president of an African country. I got to meet her, and she signed her biography for me.) He pulled out a chart.

"Aaaagh!!" I reasoned after a brief look. "I knew this would happen." I continued with my explanation of events and bragged about my recognition of the old EKG. This director had been around long enough to both hear my story without raising his eyebrows and also to believe me. You can't win.

The heart offers lots of opportunities for losing in the ED. MIs can be tricky to diagnose, arrythmia treatments may involve dangerous drugs or shocking people, and sudden deterioration without warning may occur. In the next case, I got really nervous about the outcome although I was merely a spectator.

A nurse was given the job of connecting the pacer wires to an external power source. (I was just observing as a resident. I guess this was a transvenous pacer?). She was near the foot of the bed. The cardiologist was near the head of the bed. I can't recall what he was doing. He was fiddling with something. But I can recall watching the monitor as the patient went flatline.

'Hook him up," said the cardiologist in a normal, conversational tone.

The nurse tried. And tried. Then tried some more. She was trying to slide the two male wire connectors into sockets on the small device. I could feel the nurse feel all the eyes on her fumbling fingers. The cardiologist began a torrent of "encouraging words." Pre-quoting the colleague in a prior story, "I'm glad it wasn't me," was what I said in my head.

The unconscious patient was still flatlined, and he himself began to take note of this. At first, he just lay there, quietly asleep as his heart was not beating. This changed when his neck twisted to the right and he arched his back in what looked like preparation for a seizure.

The nurse got the two leads in. The monitor began beeping regularly, the patient's head turned back forward, and he relaxed into his bed. If that nurse ever writes a book, I bet she'll remember *this* story.

The worst stories, the ones that stick the most and make you swear each time you recall them, are about the ones that got away. Fishermen tell tales of big fish they almost caught. The "almost" is the thing.

This elderly man was in 3D; you may recall that's the same room as the GI cocktail lady. He was complaining of hot flashes. His EKG showed a couple of PVCs;[44] but everything else on it was normal, at least acutely. Chronically, the patient had prostate cancer and was undergoing treatment.

As a matter of fact, he had just stopped taking the female hormone medications that were part of this cancer regimen.

"Could that be giving him hot flashes for the past day?" I asked his urologist.

"Sure," was the reply.

I was still worried about the PVCs. He was having one every so often, maybe one a minute. His cardiac enzymes were normal (troponins didn't exist back then), but . . .

"They're just PVCs, McAnon. I'll see him in the office," was the cardiologist's answer.

I never saw the patient have his "hot flashes," but he described them exactly as the nurses did who sat in our "menopause chair," the one that got the constant A/C flow.

I sent the old man home. The dissenting voices in my head were not audible until the man came back a few hours later with an MI. Then, unhelpfully, those thoughts said, "I told you so."

Now, when the MI was obvious, these voices were speaking loudly and convinced everyone in the room in my head with their clarity of reasoning.

"Dadgummit! I knew it!" (I still feel regret twenty-five years later.) Any vague misgivings get crystallized into certainty, but

---

[44] Premature Ventricular Contractions. Usually not a problem, but can become one and can be hints of real problems.

since this certainty arrives too late, it only disapproves. When it counts and there is time to act on them, those voices are barely audible; when it's too late, you can't hear anything else.

To minimize these episodes, listen hard for the minority view. Make sure you are not annoyed, or upset, or distracted. When that all fails, you just have to attack the "I told you so" with "Well, you need to speak up if you want to be heard."

Another Jedi mind trick I employ to avoid "I told you so" is as follows. I will have to give you a hypothetical (but entirely realistic) scenario. Let's say the patient gives the following answer to, "What's the problem?"

"I was moving my ex's furniture last week and I must have pulled something. I told her that couch was too heavy, she should just trash it. Well, I was OK after that, you know I'm in good shape . . .blah blah . . . so this week, I felt the soreness in my muscles, you know. I started getting an ache here (jiggling his left pectoral). My legs are a little sore, and so are my arms, especially my left one. I feel fine otherwise, I just need the pain to go away."

His workup gives us no obvious further clues.

My Jedi trick is to shrink the whole story down into the tale that will be told in the hospital halls in the event I send the guy home alive, but he comes back dead.

The halls will buzz with: "McAnon sent this forty-year-old with dull chest pain radiating to his left arm home! He came back dead! Can you believe it? What was he thinking?"

I condense complicated cases to one-liners like "pregnant girl with pleuritic pain," or "Forty-year-old man with radiating chest pain." I like to apply this scenario often and frequently use it several times a shift. At least you won't miss the board question patients.

You mostly want to avoid making mistakes that all the other doctors in your category would not make. Hard things are hard, but in the ED, even easy things can be made hard. You have to take active steps to avoid pitfalls.

I have had one other episode that involved me missing out on the counsel of my wise but too soft-spoken inner voice. (I'm sure there are dozens of cases I can't recall.) This episode is too recent for me to recount here; you are not missing anything really interesting, I just want to make a couple of points.

The "I told you so" factor was great is this case. It involved several warning signs that I noted and chose to ignore. The reasons I did this seemed smart to me at the time, but as soon as things went badly, my stubborn optimism was obvious. This clarity occurs too late, of course, after the pessimists were demonstrably proven correct.

Additionally galling is the fact that on my better days things would have been different. This man would probably still have died, but at least it would not have been when I was trying to send him home.

You cannot always be at your best. Large organizations are always cheering "excellence" and "exceptional" and "we're the best," but in reality, those titles can ever really only be applied to the very few. Everyone in the place can't be "exceptional." Even the exceptional can't always be so. It is dangerous to count on it when making decisions. Plan your systems based on average performance.

Personally, you cannot count on it, either. You will have good days and bad days. I have saved some lives in tricky scenarios that I think most other doctors would not have succeeded in. I have also made mistakes that the last fellow in my med school class wouldn't make (unless he was also having a bad day).

You cannot always judge yourself against the exceptional crowd, even if at times you may join them. "If only the best birds sang, the woods would be silent." These words hold lots of healing power.

Once I had a patient with a jaw dislocation. These patients typically appear with the mouth stuck open. I saw this case in the olden days, before we used the good sedation medications, so the relocation procedure was a good bit of trouble, but successful. The patient was now sitting in 18A with her mouth comfortably closed.

There was also some possibility of a neck injury, so now that she was in less pain, I sent her around for neck x-rays. These involve an "open mouth odontoid view," and, as you will now find it to be the obvious outcome, she popped her jaw back out.

On a good day, I would have foreseen this and picked another view or study. But this was an average day—count on them.

Assorted Cases

Case 1. As a resident, a nurse saved me from the opposite of a save when I tried to order too much lidocaine. I was just starting out as a resident. I was handwriting ICU orders for a medication and dutifully reproducing the dosage numbers straight from my spiral bound "D.C. Manual." (Note the book name change to avoid hassles.)

The nurse's brain had the better editor because my book had a misplaced decimal. I had written down ten times the correct dose.

Case 2. This is not really a case. A psychiatrist once told me of the best tattoo he had ever seen. A man had "LOVE" spelled out across the top of the fingers on one hand, and "HAT" on the other side. The man was missing a pinkie.

10

Minds

"You're gorgeous," she gushed as she gazed very intently at me, brown eyes pleading her case. She laid back onto her bed and beckoned me, focusing only on me. She had picked *me* and was blind to the six bright blue-uniformed officers surrounding the bed. However, I clearly saw the police. They had an overwhelming effect on the mood for me, but I still felt a little sad I had to transfer this friendly face to the psych facility.

This lady really liked me. I don't get called gorgeous every day—or any day (but that doesn't mean it's not true). To make things worse, my wife has confirmed several times that she would not try to catch me even if only one officer was present.

"Ten and two!" is a common cry in the ER. It refers to medications that have been used for years in ERs to control dangerously unruly patients. Ten milligrams of Haldol and two milligrams of Ativan are usually effective in calming a severely psychotic patient. Yells of "Ten and two!" are accompanied by a converging crowd of all sorts, hopefully including several security guards. Lots of interesting things occur at these times.

The Possession

This guy was huge. He was clearly very disturbed, sweaty and psychotic. Drugs or mental illness or both. His smaller brother-in-law was soothing and trying to coax him into cooperating. It was obvious the man was barely in control of himself, that this control was lessening, and that he could explode at any second.

"Ten and two!"

As the crowd of us stood nearby, trying to talk him down, the brother-in-law got right up in his face, stroking him and talking to him like he was a three-hundred-pound baby with precocious muscles. We were all waiting for the nurse to retrieve the Haldol and Ativan.

The near-boiling, more like, the ready-to-explode, patient noticed the syringe and began pleading with us not to stick him with a needle.

He turned to his brother-in-law with abnormal passion: "Don't let them stick me! Please don't let them stick me!" he cried, repeatedly and piteously in a high-pitched, infantile voice. One instinct he aroused in us was to pick him up and rock him to sleep. Of course, other instincts, such as "Run away!" were also in play, because the man's face was contorted with scary, wide-eyed expressions indicating extreme volatility. Our fear was compounded by the fact that if we did want to pick him up to calm him, we would need a forklift.

The in-law was a real hero in trying to calm the patient down as we began planning our D-Day. This brave soul was putting himself in harm's way, between us and the patient, trying desperately to talk "the Hulk" down.

The medical team slowly advanced on the bed, constantly reassuring verbally, but not agreeing to any "no medication" pleas. With medications ready, we pounced.

At least six souls divided up his extremities, head, and torso, and we all held him down against the bed, concentrating on holding his thigh motionless so the nurse could inject him.

The needle went through his blue jeans when an otherworldly, guttural voice slowly croaked:

"You let 'em stick me, brother-in-law." He glared with rage at our hero. He repeated this over and over, in a growl that reverberated as if we were in Tomb 3B instead of ED room 3B.

The abrupt and striking changes in his voice and expression were similar to those horror movie demonic possessions. As a matter of fact, one of our techs ran terrified from the room. She did not stop until she reached a bathroom, where she was found praying for protection against the demon.

The Haldol and Ativan exorcised his demon, and he was soon sleeping like a baby.

Ativan alone can work wonders. It is addictive and can be abused, so it has to be used with caution, but it is our main go-to drug for prolonged seizures or stimulant psychosis.

Impressive Ativan Abuse

The radio report was of a seizure patient coming in, and EMS was requesting Ativan. It was a long trip, so another call came in later, requesting repeated Ativan. The patient was continuing to seize.

Still seizing on arrival, we had an official status epilepticus patient, with a prolonged grand mal seizure. She was a woman in her twenties, unresponsive and jerking rhythmically and violently on the bed. I treated her by the book, with incrementally increasing doses of the benzodiazepine as the main therapy. I had worked up to eight milligrams of Ativan before she finally stopped seizing. Now she seemed too drowsy to protect her airway.

I intubated her trachea without difficulty, with no other medications necessary. She was out. The RT placed her on the ventilator, and she lay peacefully asleep, postictal and eyes closed. She and I and the nurses were taking a breath after the drama of the seizures, and all was quiet for several minutes.

Until Nurse G. walked in:

"I know this girl! She has fake seizures. She's addicted to benzos and she fakes seizures to get them."

The patient's eyes popped wide open. My eyes probably also widened, as I was at the head of the bed and looking straight at her when this happened. She was very awake, lying on her back with the large ET tube protruding from her mouth. The next sequence of events happened within a minute.

"Blink your eyes three times," I instructed.

She did just that, clearly and deliberately. Her eyes remained opened and she was very alert.

I quickly deflated the balloon and pulled the tube out.

She coughed once or twice, cleared her throat and started yelling a little hoarsely, "I do too have real seizures! These are real seizures! That nurse is lying! I have real seizures!"

I was impressed.

I think this patient was intentionally, consciously faking a seizure to get the medication she desired or was addicted to.

I saw a similar, but not quite as remarkable a case.

This man was not responding and was jerking in a bizarre manner. Now, grand mal seizure patients may move in dramatic or odd ways, but this patient was convulsing in a pattern that did not fit normal movement, nor did it fit a typical seizure.

We call these nonepileptic seizures. "Pseudo-seizures" is the "old" word some reasonably consider pejorative. I say reasonable and you will understand soon.

The "seizing" man was continuing his behavior while I discussed him with his two sisters standing at the bedside. It seems he was under their care, living with them, and making $1,200/month (in the 1990s) in disability due to a brain tumor and seizures.

I attempted to inform the sisters that what was occurring today was not seizures caused by a tumor. I was having difficulty convincing them. The patient was jerking violently throughout this long discussion, with an occasional brief pause seemingly timed so that he could better hear us talk.

"Whatever he is doing now is not due to seizures or a tumor. It may be anxiety, or he may be even trying to manipulate you."

I continued this discussion for several minutes. The sisters were extremely concerned and kept asking questions, forcing me to repeat myself.

I was startled when the man sat up, said, "I don't have to listen to this anymore," pulled out his IV and walked out of the ED.

One of the sisters asked me, "Did his brain tumor make him do that?"

Well, certain tumors can affect your personality and judgement, so maybe. But the seizure-like activity and his sudden stop had to have been volitional. He was intentionally up to something. I think he was giving pseudo-seizures a bad name. He was having a pseudo-pseudo-seizure. It is a little tricky.

Warning: No evidence-based care is described in the following paragraphs. I have run my own pseudo-experiments, but these will meet no one's standards.

There are those who truly fake seizures for money, sympathy, drugs—for who knows what. It is reasonable to have a less-than-charitable stance towards these patients, and many healthcare workers do.

There are others, unfairly stigmatized, who have "fake" seizures. These are the true pseudo-seizures or non-epileptic seizures. While many think this behavior is under the conscious control of the patient, I do not.

I think this behavior is most consistent with those "twilight of the consciousness" behaviors like hypnosis, sleeping, coughing, yawning, crying, or laughing. These behaviors are only sort-of under self-control. I clump these pseudo-seizures with other conversion disorder behaviors, like psychogenic weakness or paralysis or catatonic spells. It's self-hypnosis.

Regardless, I think it pays to have a nonjudgmental attitude towards these patients, if only for the sake of improving the flow of patients. I have a couple of tricks that has made living with these patients in the ED easier.

First, if it looks like a seizure, it is OK to treat it like one. A seizure deserves Ativan, and so does anxiety bad enough to make you act so bizarre that your behavior is easily confused with a seizure.

Another trick is to allow for "face saving" and give a path back to normalcy. Pretend like you are a hypnotist on an antimatter planet. Hypnotize them back to normal behavior.

"These smelling salts should stop the seizure. Hah! Now she's moving normally; she should stop jerking soon."

"Ah! I just saw the leg move when I pinched it; she should start moving better now." Be creative. This works fairly often. If not, Ativan and a couple of hours of chilling generally cure the harder cases.

Catatonia is reportedly a very rare psychiatric condition where the patient remains frozen, in a fixed position, and nontalking. I say "reportedly" because such behavior is extremely common in ERs.

Maybe it's pseudo-catatonia. Whatever, I've already passed my last boards. Anyway, the patient I am discussing will be lying or sitting motionless and not talking. They will seem to have no "real" reason to be unable to act alert. This condition is common after overdoses that are more "cries for help," or pseudo-overdoses.

Unlike the pseudo-pseudo seizures, who are clearly in control of their behavior, I think most of these catatonic patients are not in true volitional control. They are self-hypnotized in a state of varying degrees of immobility.

The patient's facial expression, frequently lying on a bed with a frozen, concerned expression, eyebrows a little furrowed with a vertical crease in the forehead, will give you one clue. Another trick is to touch the eyelashes; there will frequently be a little pseudo-blink.

Lots of patients will learn this trick of ours and no longer respond this way, so you may have just one shot. The part of the brain that's in control may not be that "person," but it may still be smart. *Note: The delusional part of one's brain may be clever, even if unwise.*

Once you feel comfortable that the patient is not dangerously unresponsive, it's frequently possible to connect with the suppressed normalcy. I better expand on that voodoo.

To explain myself more easily, I'll relate a composite, pseudo-patient. I have had such encounters dozens of times, but none come to mind individually.

The pseudo-patient was lying motionless on the bed. She had just overdosed on ten amoxicillin tablets and was not responsive. As the consummate medical professional, I doubted that the Amoxil could produce such sedation.

Her eyelids fluttered a little, from the strain of being held shut. I touched her lash and her eyelids tightened a little.

"Hmmm, this looks like a cocaine overdose," I said with authority.

The patient's lips moved, but no sound came out. I continued repeating dosages of the same or similar pronouncements. "Yep, cocaine, or maybe meth." Was that a whisper?

I persisted and the patient increased the vigor of her response, I encouraged any sign of alertness, "Ah, she's coming back, the cocaine isn't . . ."

"I didn't use cocaine!" The newly clear voice indicated to me that the patient would now be more cooperative and would be much easier to assess. I may have saved her a few thousand dollars and a bunch of radiation or even an intubation.

For pseudo-seizures or pseudo-catatonia, variations of these "treatments" are extremely useful. Here are a few underlying principles. Use something shocking, like accusations of cocaine use, to arouse the suppressed normalcy. Follow this with encouraging any remotely normal behavior by giving face-saving paths back to the real world.

Avoid things that create any further investment in whatever the patient is doing that could cause problems. If the patient (or the deluded sub-personality) senses hostility or judgmentalism, they will frequently double down and increase their abnormal behavior.

Note: It may be important to pre-inform any surrounding family members of your intentions. If they are aware you are trying to avoid an extensive, expensive, potentially harmful workup or treatment of someone with pseudo-altered mental status, the family will let you get away with this pseudo-abusive behavior.

Water Allergy

Some patients are easy. They come pre-diagnosed. This lady was sent to us by the state psychiatric facility, so we had a heads-up. This woman was sent to be treated for dehydration. She was refusing to drink anything, and this was her third day of such behavior.

"I'm allergic to water," was her explanation. Cool.

I retrieved a marker, a syringe filled with sterile water, and a fairly self-controlled nurse.

"That would be very unusual, so we'll need to confirm this with a skin test," I said, careful not to overdo the professionalism.

I drew a little circle on her forearm, got ready with the syringe. The nurse positioned herself nearby.

With an arm wave across the department, buzzing with activity, I reassured her. "We've got everything here to treat allergic reactions, so this is the best place to do this."

I carefully placed a small drop of water in the center of the drawn circle, as the patient intensely focused on the spot.

She and I saw the same immediate response: nothing. She was a little startled by the nothing, but I was not. Nothing happens all the time, day in and day out.

The three of us observed her arm for a few minutes and there was also no delayed response. After I declared her not allergic to water, the patient eagerly accepted water, apple juice, and the best we had to offer: cranberry juice.

Other easy cases include the lady with long curls of white hair. She shouted in anger at her fellow patient, "Stop calling me Santa Claus. I'm Dolly Parton!"

Some psychiatric (or not?) patients are hard.

The gentleman was seated in 3B. He was seated as you should be in a hospital bed and looked self-confident in his erect posture and tweed coat. The chart said he was here for medical clearance to the state psychiatric hospital. The referring facility was asking for help because they couldn't get him to eat, and the psychiatric facility wouldn't take him unless he stopped by our ED to be checked.

He looked polished as he asked, "How are you?" or some such pleasantry when I entered the room.

I was scanning him for signs of mental illness and coming up empty. This man seemed pretty normal. He was a professor from a nearby city. He relayed, with some intensity, that he had been unfairly treated in some personnel dispute at the college. Certain private emails had been made not private, and that was the real issue here. He reassured me, "I am not homicidal or suicidal, I am having no hallucinations or difficulty thinking. I am just standing up for myself."

Why wasn't he eating? "I am protesting for computer privacy. I am on a hunger strike."

I talked with him for quite a while, trying to decide if this guy was a legitimate hunger-striker or if I should deem him mentally unwell enough to justify forcibly treating him. (He was refusing electrolyte tests or IV fluids.)

The tie-breaking question for me came to mind. "Who knows about this hunger strike? Who have you told?"

"Only you," he answered.

Hmmm. "Well, I think that a real protestor wants someone to know that he is protesting. What's the point if it's a secret?

That can't help change anything. I'm going to have to say that it's my call to force you to get treatment."

He continued to act as a perfect gentleman as we treated his dehydration then shipped him off.

10 and 2!

Ten and two! Those words ring in the memories of anyone who has worked in an ED for more than a few days. Ten milligrams of Haldol and two of Ativan have exorcised spirits, dethroned kings, removed presidents, made aliens disappear, and added greatly to the general peace.

The desire to help, paychecks, and morbid curiosity compel crowds of us to run to the source of the sirens song, "We need ten and two."

These situations are almost always urgent enough that the meds are injected through clothing. (I've never seen an infection in thousands of sticks, although surely, they have occurred.) There are usually several security guards or police holding extremities.

In the old days, security was light, and the male nurses were important in running down or controlling these patients. Security guards were not always around, and the ED staff was frequently overpowered by these psychotic folks.

Only twice in my career have I had to pull out the medical nuclear option: succinylcholine. This drug causes paralysis of everything within just a few minutes, even those necessary to breathe, so intubation is essential. (These days I would probably use large doses of ketamine instead of succ.)

Of these two cases, that is all I remember. I paralyzed and intubated them. Something else had to have happened next, but as evidence of the striking nature of the ED experience, those cases do not even rise to "here's a few more details." Actually, I now recall that one of them was an ex-college football player, arms bigger that my legs, lifting off the ground the two or more nurses or police officers on each extremity.

These wild psychiatric patients liven things up and everyone working in the ED will have a story. The patients themselves create some great ones.

I remember the manic woman with the medical education describing the "satellites that shoot lasers into my urethra." Or the guy who saw hundreds of snakes attacking him (unlikely) and shot both his feet trying to kill them (moderate damage done). There was also the past-menopause lady who claimed to be pregnant with "five or six babies," as she waved her hand over her abdomen.

"What kind of babies?" I asked innocently.

"People babies, stupid." She was shocked at my cluelessness.

I typically enjoy taking care of psychiatric patients. The really psychotic often respond well to meds, and some of the more mildly afflicted don't feel bad, so they will interestingly interact with you ...

"Are you sure you should be showing a magic trick to a psych patient?" the older teen admonished me.

These patients frequently are self-aware when treated or in between psychotic breaks. This often gives them a refreshing, nonjudgmental humility. I do not typically enjoy those who come in just for a bed or food, or the patients who have been "suicidal" for over twenty years, four times a month. Many of the personality disorders are difficult to deal with.

I think I am finally "used to" the next group of patients, but I have never really enjoyed the interactions or felt myself very helpful to them.

Patients just using us to get drugs is one of the downsides of the ED job. The fear of undertreating a real sufferer is in tension with the fear of rewarding fraudulent or addictive behavior. I've had one clear victory:

I rounded with several other residents on a young man requiring pain medications for some ailment. He was getting these pain meds and being taken seriously by us. His mother happened to be hospitalized on another floor, being treated for terminal cancer and getting IV narcotics for pain.

The young man was accompanied by his wife, and I saw them several times throughout the week, as I was part of a large team caring for him. One day, the attending was informed that the man was caught stealing the narcotics from his mother's pain medication infusion. The attending immediately discharged the man.

A couple of weeks later, I was moonlighting down the road, when this same young man comes in accompanied by his "wife." Well, now she was his "sister." They did not recognize me, as I had blended in with the other residents when I rounded on him in his prior hospitalization, but I certainly recognized him and his female companion. It was no surprise that his ED complaint and listed allergies would require narcotics to treat him (due to multiple allergies, intractable pain, or some other similar issue).

"No, no recent hospitalizations," he lied to me.

It was satisfying to confront him and move him along with the certainty that he was lying. We rarely have this certainty, and treating these patients is hard work.

A few years later I ran across another couple. Numerous times. I knew this couple and they knew me. Our relationship had progressed to the point that they would ask the triage nurse if I was on duty and frequently leave if they heard my name. I had seen them in numerous situations and was certain that they were fraudulently attempting to get pain meds. The male always wore a cleric's smock. He was a Wiccan priest.

During that time in my career, I saw a young teenager with "chronic back pain, allergic to NSAIDs."[45] That struck me as a little odd. The patient herself was reasonable seeming, with a history and physical consistent with low back pain.

"You're allergic to NSAIDs?" I read from her chart. She didn't know what I was talking about. That was very odd.

The very next patient was a similar bizarre case of a young teen with all the trappings of an older adult drug seeker. Two suspicious teens at the same time? I didn't recognize their names. This was too much.

I walked up to registration and found out that both the teens were signed in by the same adult couple. The clerk pointed to this couple sitting in the waiting room, one of which was wearing a cleric's smock. I called the police due to the fact that these teenagers were being used in a fraudulent scheme, but I don't know if anything helpful happened. I never saw the teens with "adult stories" again, but I still saw the couple from time to time.

"Tell them I'll be glad to treat their pain or anything else wrong with them, but I can't give them narcotics," was my instructions to the triage nurse whenever I saw their names pop up. They typically left when hearing that news.

I have few helpful tricks in dealing with these patients. I have definitely just said "No" more often over the years based on hunches. One such patient comes to mind from the olden times, before there were state databases intended to keep track of the really abusive patients.

This patient was a nurse (so she said, she was certainly medically educated). She was from Florida, she had bleeding ulcers, her cancer pain was horrible, her pain meds ran out while she was visiting, she had to stay with her sick daughter. "Here's my doctor's number—but, oh wait—she's out of town."

---

[45] Non-Steroidal Anti-Inflammatory Drugs. Ibuprofen is one.

There were lots more details that I can't recall, and on and on it went. All the details were carefully aligned to create the perfect story to pigeonhole me into prescribing her a significant amount of narcotic.

I just said no.

As she was peacefully leaving (not a given), she asked, "Now what was it about my story that seemed suspicious?" As if she were trying to fine tune it further!

Taking care of folks with chronic pain complaints is hard. Many of them have real diseases and real pain. Many of them are total frauds and criminals. I typically err on the side of treating them in the ED and err on the side of not giving them any prescriptions. I am more concerned about them trafficking the pain meds to someone else than I am about the ethical implications of me being fooled into overtreating or enabling them.

I try hard, but treating these patients still annoys me. I sometimes return the favor and annoy them. When drug-seeking patients are asking for a specific drug, they will often pretend to not remember the name. They will say, "It starts with a 'D,' umm 'De,' maybe 'Di . . .'" I typically don't help and just wait until they get frustrated and blurt out "Dilaudid!"

We use narcotics for the severe pain that is common in ED patients. Working amongst these drugs is too much temptation for some, and rarely, a medical person succumbs.

Nurses are not immune from the temptation of these medications, and I no longer work directly with two nurse friends who developed addictions and began using ED meds. Both of them are fully rehabilitated and work in other medical areas.

Doctors are also not immune. Decades ago in my career, there were seven of us in the group. Five out of that seven were under some kind of observation for substance addiction. I was "supervising" one of the guys who was an alcoholic. He was an excellent physician, cool as a cucumber, and never showed any signs to me that he had begun drinking again until we had to fill his shifts. I suppose I was a bad supervisor.

Assorted Cases

Case 1

The male patient had a head bleed, a hemorrhagic stroke. He was nonverbal, with his eyes deviated to the left, lying motionless on bed 2A. His daughter gasped loudly when she saw his condition as she walked up to the foot of his bed. The patient moved his eyes straight forward towards his daughter and raised himself to sit upright for only a moment, then fell back, his eyes looking back to the left and not moving again as the stroke regained control.

Case 1A

The patient was an older male in 3A with a hemorrhagic stroke.[46] He was looking straight ahead, then raised his left arm as if to look at his watch. He cut his eyes to the left as you would expect, but then his eyes stayed fixed to the left, even as he lowered his arm. He never moved his eyes again.

Case 1B

The patient in 3A was floridly psychotic. He was unleashing a steady stream of agitated nonsense when he started to rise from his bed in a threatening manner, all while loudly shouting gibberish.

A security guard pulled a taser and pointed it at his chest. The out-of-control man suddenly stopped his yelling and said

---

[46] Hemorrhagic strokes are caused by too much blood in the wrong place. Most strokes are caused by not enough blood in the right place.

something like, “It’s OK, I’m good,” raised his hands a little to signify compliance, then scooted back into place on the bed. As soon as he was lying back (this was within a few seconds of saying, “I’m good”), he resumed his excited, rambling, pressured psychotic speech.

11
Souls

What if you gain the whole world, but lose your soul? That is like *the* question. It is very easy to lose your soul in the ED. First of all, just to get there you've had to do some kind of training; much of that is soul-sucking work. There are certainly no shortcuts to being an ED doctor, and the main path is hard all along the way.

Working in any capacity in EDs is bad for your health due to the long hours or strange shifts. In residency, I knew a nurse who fell asleep after a night shift, getting killed in an MVA.

Weird hours, lots of medical stress, but also lots of social stress is a problem. Spending twelve hours in confrontation or high-stakes discussions with people makes it more difficult for you to benefit from the positive social interactions from friends or family.

The ED uses you up in a way that is hard to fix. It takes me a couple of days for my work mode to melt away. Lots of very hard, physical activity or engaging hobbies helps me.

I haven't lost my soul yet, but it's sometimes as hard to find as my keys. There are tricks to keep track of those keys, and some of those techniques are helpful for souls also. Keeping things neat and using routines are helpful for both.

Probably the most important de-stressor is coming to your job prepared. Competency helps produce confidence, which helps produce calm. Go out of your way to be as competent as possible.

My residency occurred in a time now gone, with more opportunities to learn early. There was a cost to that. But it was a necessary cost.

It is essential to become competent in what you are planning to do. It is also essential to test yourself to make sure you're up to the task as early as is feasible. Check the boat for leaks before you get far offshore.

My residency offered opportunities in both training and testing. We all took ACLS, PALS, ATLS[47] early on and were encouraged to moonlight.

As a real MD, with my brand-new license, I would do shifts in small ERs for experience and money. I only went to the tiny areas where I would likely get plenty of sleep, to avoid hurting my performance of residency duties. One place, now gone, had a surgeon listed whose privileges included: general surgery, vascular surgery, and neurosurgery!

These hospitals were always happy to get us residents. (It must have been hard for them to provide coverage.) The staff usually fed us, got us a bed, and would make non-critical patients wait for periods so we could have chunks of sleep time. There were certainly benefits, but there were also some unique challenges in these rural areas.

In one case, I had worked the patient up and made my decision. I put in the request to talk to the lady's primary provider. When he returned the call, I gave him my brief presentation: the description of her complaint, exam, workup, and diagnosis. In this case, severe congestive heart failure was the problem.

"Mrs. Jones always says she can't breathe," resisted her primary doctor. Even if true, things were different on this day. The x-ray showed a lot of new pulmonary edema.

---

[47] Advanced Cardiac Life Support, Pediatric Advanced Life Support and Advanced Trauma Life Support. These are all algorithm heavy classes that many jobs require.

“She needs to be admitted; she can’t always have this much fluid in her lungs,” I countered.

“Fine, *you* admit her.” And so, I did. Hopefully her doctor was more reasonable when he saw her in person. This was not a typical case, but some of the isolated doctors worked in a different, more risk-taking world back then.

One night of moonlighting, I saw a guy brought in wailing in the back of a pickup truck. His forearm was the size of a football from the shattered bone, muscle damage, and hematoma caused by the .45 caliber pistol. Ten milligrams of morphine IV put him to sleep. If I awakened him by shaking his shoulder (on the not-shot side), he was in immediate and severe pain. If I left him alone, he was snoring and sedated enough to make me nervous.

In another tiny ED, a moderately sick small infant needed a lumbar puncture. While performing this, I was pleased by the number of surrounding individuals that were there to help. Unhelpfully, after obtaining the sample, I was told, “We can’t run this in the middle of the night.” No problem, we just transferred the fluid with the baby to the bigger hospital.

Residencies are designed to teach as you are given more and more responsibility. Any role in medicine benefits from this approach. I recall several teaching moments such as:

“What do you see?” the kind but still scary surgeon asked me, when I had been a resident less than a week.

“A pneumothorax on the right,” I answered quickly, but not confidently because I sensed there must be some trap. The x-ray was obvious, and I was still looking for some subtle abnormality when he popped up another film on the view box.

“Right pneumothorax,” again easy.

He slapped up another film after removing the last one.

“Another pneumothorax, smaller than the others.” I was looking very hard to see what the trick was as he was moving films around quickly.

"And a central line in place," I added. Maybe that was what he wanted to hear. He stuck up another film.

I had to look a little while before I finally spotted it. "A tiny right pneumothorax and a central line.[48]"

Now I got it. Reading that film was one of my very first duties as a resident. Someone on the night shift had put in a line, and I was the one that was to check the film for the complication of a pneumothorax. I had missed it, and the surgeon was dramatically pointing this out to me.

I did not feel too bad because others following me (including a radiologist) had misread the same film, and even one of the more obvious later pneumos,[49] but the surgeon's lesson clearly had an impact. One: I have not missed a pneumo since (that I know of) and have spotted some pretty subtle ones. Two: I still remember the episode.

All of these varied experiences early on taught me and tested me so that I was prepared, and knew it, for the career I was taking. Competence and confidence are both essential.

There are some other aspects to soul-keeping. A real life outside medicine is extremely helpful. You need a whole other world, with different values, pecking orders, rewards, and punishments. Families, hobbies, charity work, something that engages you. I take advantage of several of these self-contained worlds in all of these areas.

Realize that medicine, like I suppose every career, will try to absorb you for itself alone. Every career is like the alien "Blob." It would seem to be easy to outrun it, but this creeping mass was somehow able to eat half the town.

---

[48] This would have been a subclavian central line. They show up on x-ray because a small radio-opaque stripe is manufactured into them. A known complication of them is a pneumothorax.

[49] See how nice it is too shorten these long words when the context allows? Most of these long words are not just jargon. They are necessary for precision.

The work-life balance is hard to maintain. Something as mundane as "scheduling" will eat at your very soul:

I knew that you have to watch out for your own soul to help others. I had a good family and I wanted to be a good family member. I was all set to attend my aunt's funeral. I had spent more time with her than my other aunts and still am in close contact with her children. I was glad I was going to get to go until ... another ED doctor's grandmother died.

We talked about it and decided his case for getting off was stronger than mine.

Although I have had lots of time off, I still miss lots of things. No regular meetings, no clubs, nothing predictable is possible with my schedule.

I was working a shift and had just begun the care of a critical patient with an MI, when my wife checked into L&D, appropriately expanded at term with my unborn daughter. It was my last shift for several days, so the lucky timing was looking good, but it still added a lot of stress to the situation.

I have missed lots of things that I, or those close to me, wanted me to do. I have minimized this by building in some margin, by working fewer shifts than I could have, avoiding some opportunities offered, and not angling for notoriety within the medical community.

I advise everyone within earshot (No one ever asks, I have to force my advice upon them): avoid as much debt as possible to prevent getting trapped into working too much, just say "no" a lot, never give 100% unless it is a dire emergency. Always have some reserve fuel available.

Stress is obviously toxic to souls, especially the constant, repetitive stuff. As I mentioned earlier, anything you can relegate to the routine helps with this, just like keeping up with keys by always placing them in the same spot.

The mentally ill are frequently experts in deploying mind tricks against whatever is assailing them. They have much to teach us.

I let the obsessive-compulsive parts of my brain take over the task of getting ready for work. Partly because those inner urges will be the least assuaged in the chaotic ED. Same scrubs, same coat, same shoe covers.

Once at work, I try to identify which tasks, situations and people *de-stress* me as well as those that *distress* me. This is pretty hard to predict and certainly varies tremendously among individuals.

During a shift, I do not like discussing hard medical stories that are not my current problem. I like to talk about outside events. If things are slow, in the middle of the night, I might engage in a hard political or philosophical discussion. More commonly, I engage in several conversations simultaneously, reduced to a sentence at a time when we pass each other while working.

Almost everyone in the ED is under stress. Most of the situations command seriousness, but you don't have to *act* serious. The important things are compelling and easy to focus on by all. It is harder to lighten back up when the situation allows. People, including myself, tend to get stuck in this intense seriousness. Therefore, I try to de-stress the whole place.

I tease everyone. Pestering housekeeping, lab, maintenance—whoever shows up. I like to play tricks on nurses in particular, and there is no telling how many lives they have saved by letting me offload my stress.

I self-medicate with humor (by my definition, ignore the nurse detractors). I typically have a "schtick" at work where I act like a grumpy tightwad doctor who is one of the few who understands the evil of nurses.

In the ED, humor is easy. There is such a chance of sadness or horror nearby that the worst joke may be enough provocation for a smile or laugh. It's like a Hollywood star who gets lots of praise for occasionally acting like a normal person; the bar for what is considered humor is low in the ED.

I joke about nurses' "seances" instead of meetings, the nurses' "lair," instead of lounge. When greeting nurses, I'll say: "Hello, ladies," using air quotes. You get it. Or maybe you don't. But just remember, teamwork is essential—it's just that there is a Team Doctor and a Team Nurse. "Nurse" rhymes with "curse," "perverse," and "adverse." That can't be a coincidence.

Being around young coworkers also helps. They laugh, joke and play. They teach me new words. It is important to keep in touch with those of a different age than yourself.

My wife has had by far the most impact on my soul. Seriously. But I frequently make jokes about her at work. I may bring her up as "my unemployable English-major wife." This unemployability is of course, not true. I partly do this in an attempt to indirectly support the working mothers' feelings.

I make jokes at my wife's expense all the time that are unfair, unreasonable, and usually the precise opposite of my true feelings. It might make my home life easier overall if I did not tell such spousal jokes, but I am in too deep now. Here are a few examples:

Joke 1. Me: "I have been married twenty happy years."

Nurse: "Wait, Dr. M., you've been married longer than that."

Me: "Well, thirty-seven years total; twenty happy ones."

Nurse: "Hahaha! So, the last ones are happy?"

Me: "It's a day-to-day thing."

Joke 2. "Today's my anniversary! No, wait. It's Pearl Harbor day. I knew it was something."

Joke 3. "This ring is a symbol of the noose around my neck."

I also know several high-quality non-spouse jokes. I cannot tell the horrifically inappropriate jokes the pediatric nurse (she looks like a normal human being, however . . .) told me, but I can tell this joke. I did not make it up, the joke I mean. This is not a true story:

"This man was driving down the interstate. His wife calls him on the cell phone, 'Hey honey, some idiot is driving the wrong way down the interstate.' The man replied, 'There's not just one, there's hundreds of them!'"

All doctors know lots of lawyer jokes. My favorite one: The woman was paying her lawyer for the will he had just drawn up. "That'll be a hundred dollars," he said.

She laid a crisp hundred-dollar bill on the desk and turned to leave. The lawyer picked up the bill and immediately noticed that the lady had accidently left him two bills, stuck together.

Now the lawyer was faced with an ethical decision: "Should I keep both bills . . . or split the money with my partner?"

I am not the only one with jokes. The best prank on me deserves a paragraph or two. This is a true story:

I was paying for gas at the counter. The pump wouldn't take my card, it was 2:30 a.m., I had just finished a hard shift, I was ready to go to sleep. I was still in my scrubs.

The cute little girl noticed the scrubs and looked up at me from her eight-year-old height.

"Are you a doctor?" she looked so concerned.

"Yes," I said. I knew that was the wrong answer, but what could I do?

"Please come quick, I think my mom is having a baby."

I was struggling to get back into work mode, muttering a little. I ran out with the little girl to find her mother in the ambulance, in the front seat, laughing and dressed in her EMS uniform.

Nurses have jokes, too. One nurse had this routine she used to make fun of me. There is absolutely no truth to the accusation contained in her skit, but she was pretty funny with: "Hello, I'm Dr. M. Your wife has died. Do you want to see a magic trick?" Because of the horrendous accusation contained therein, I spent lots of time trying to defend myself to her laughing audience.

I might have subtly avoided hugging family members (I always at least pat them) and talked a little fast, but I never did a magic trick in the family room.

In these "death talks," it is my opinion that you should avoid beating around the bush or going on a long, meandering monologue before getting to "passed away." The look on their faces as you begin to talk indicates that every second in delay is torturous to them.

I was taken aback by a neurosurgeon's "tone deafness" when he went to inform a family of something horrendous. He walked in the room, sniffed a few times, and asked, "Do any of you have allergies? I do." Before anyone could answer, he was giving them bad news.

There are times when some comments are just not quite right, and certainly times when jokes are decidedly inappropriate. Right now, while you are reading this book, is not one of those times.

I tried to sell my college-age son to nursing students for years. I would offer them a dollar amount to marry him (based on tuition I was paying), then state, "He also comes with a Camry, with a new engine."

My favorite answer from a student was a clarifying question: "How many miles on the car?"

I am also not the only doctor who tries to use humor therapeutically. A long-time friend and colleague told us of this episode minutes after it happened. He was talking to a patient and the topic of where she worked came up. She worked for a doctor who is well-known for being a bear.

Dr S—, in an attempt at forming comradery with the patient asked, "How can you possibly work for that man?"

The patient's reply was, "He's my father."

You can't win.

Training, routines, and humor help with stress, but it also helps to have thought it all through: to have some overall sense of meaning or structure; to be at peace with reality.

Religion is a powerful tool for saving souls. My own helped me greatly by spurring me to take water to the prisoners, be charitable to those that despised me, forgive a lot and judge a little. These things are not small at all and helped me and those I treated or worked with.

The comforts of religion can also be powerful, especially assurances about being cared for now as well as promises of better things to come. Although I have lost much of religion's comfort over the years, my little flame of faith getting blown about by winds in the long night, there is still reason to hope, and we modern folk should not too quickly dismiss the wisdom of the past.

In my world in the U.S., we have lost any broader, comforting cultural view. I am pained as I write by all the cultural divisions our country is experiencing now, how smart people reach such different conclusions while sorting through the same facts. It hurts me to argue online with Dr. McNemesis, who I rarely seem to be able to agree with on anything nonmedical. (I am always right, but he always "wins" when he calls me "boomer.")

As I said in earlier parts of the book, everyone lives in a glass house. No one should be throwing stones. *Laceration Pearl: Get rid of any glass tables around, to avoid lots of suturing.*

The problem of suffering is a hard nut to crack, and I have never run across any answer that really works well at all times. You solve one mystery, you create another. From a totally in-charge God, to a mindless meaninglessness, there is a whole range of solutions that aren't fully comforting in the ED universe.

I think that the best stance is to offer compassion and grace towards the fellow human beings around you, both the patients and coworkers. We are all clueless losers trying to make our way through life, all needing help and guidance.

Don't get me wrong; just because I see problems in the current answers to these questions, it doesn't mean I suggest giving up looking for them. Every little whisper about meaning you hear is worth a careful listening.

Here is another trick we can learn from the mentally ill. Psychotics frequently find meaning in odd places. "Ideas of reference" is one of these: "Look on the TV. Halle Berry is staring at *me!"* for example. The search for meaning in reality isn't what makes you insane, it's how you conduct that search.

The fact that the most fractured minds around see meaning everywhere and in all the wrong places indicates that our brains are designed to search for it and rewarded when we find meaning.

Meaning soothes the soul. Use your metal detector and scan life's beach, saving every trinket you find. Every once in a while, the "beep" means gold. A little meaning goes a long way in keeping your soul alive and kicking.

The ED offers a unique vantage point at times. I have seen a few things that feel like they have some importance in these questions of meaning. Some insights gained at work (or these tales) may help with soul maintenance.

I have seen several old souls, stricken literally with strokes, stuck in bed with limbs frozen in contractures, and being fed through gastric tubes respond to my questions with: "Fine. I'm doing great. I feel fine!"

What? People and their brains are weird and astoundingly resilient, but, what? What does that mean? How can these bed-bound patients, essentially imprisoned in the nursing home, be cheerful and happy to carry on?

In the ED we are often given glimpses of souls laid bare; shouldn't we learn something from that? I do not know what to make of all the horror, the plane crash, the babies, the families. What do you do with all that? If there is any positive effect on my soul, it is to make me cling tighter to things that soothe, to the moment, to children, to the creation, to those I love.

It's All a Matter of Life and Death

This very young wife had collapsed against me in her grief. We were seated in the family room, she was on my right side and several family members were seated across from me, stunned into silence. The room was small and bleak. It did not appear to be designed by human beings for human beings dealing with such matters. I was not finding fault, everyone had tried hard, I was not placing any blame. I couldn't build a room. I couldn't even find suitably human words to use for the task at hand.

Although all these families already know the blow that is coming, denial holds them in suspension until you get to the potent final word. Dead. Passed away. Died. Whichever you pick, it's the wrong word, but less final words will not do.

This was years ago, and I had a young wife at the time. She and the woman crumpled beside me were not unalike. My wife always seemed to be too tender for this world, designed for a much kinder place, as did the wife whose husband just died. (Should I have used "passed away"?)

Her soft sobs grew stronger. The several faces across from me were now hidden behind hands, tears running through fingers.

She was sinking into grief and pulling the rest of us down with her. I would survive afloat—I was only briefly connected to these lives, but I wasn't sure about the others. I had teary eyes, but besides myself, everyone in the room was melting, crying, drowning, when:

"My contact fell out," she sniffled.

What was this? The rest of the room sniffed once or twice and joined her on the floor, searching the floor with their hands, grief suddenly becalmed.

"Is this it? Look under the chair. It's gotta be close."

What was that all about? Who knows? People are amazing; never underestimate them. In addition to a proper respect for the weirdness of humanity, I suggest that the vignette above illustrates one of the most effective healers for the soul: the constant current of Life itself. Life is like the rivers that dry to a slow trickle in one season, then swell to raging floods the next; either way, the water is always steadily moving in its downhill course. The flow never stops, nor does Life.

That is not how we imagine it, especially when we consider Life in its tragic form. The young-in-the-ways of-suffering imagine it like the ending of the movie *Gallipoli,* where time stands still with the tragedy of the young soldier's death, caught in mid stride, frozen as the eternal death of a wasted young man.

But slow down, take your time, and just imagine a little longer. This shot-up young man would continue his forward momentum and fall. Others around him would, too. Eventually, others would come and retrieve the bodies, and soon the battlefield would revert to desert, the beetles would come out, a flower would bloom, some bright little bird would flit by.

That would ruin the movie, but that's what life does. It diminishes the horror, at least a little, by moving on. By adding new characters. The mother dies, but the baby survives. The brother dies, but the sister lives on; the husband dies, but the wife lives on. She grieves, she grows, she mourns, she raises her children, she marries . . . This truth is hard to see at times and should rarely be pointed out to those fresh in grief.

The amount and length of grief is directly proportional to the amount of change to your brain structure that person has affected. Pathways and connections laid down over years, intertwining memories and emotions, have to be rewired, bypassed, rerouted. Time slowly flows through the brain; eroding, reshaping, and cleansing.

It's a matter of Life and Death. Everything is. Always. For my part, I just accept that that is the way it is. I soothe my soul by reminding myself that as Time marches on, she heals along the way. I remember the plane crash and the death and the thousands of other sadnesses, but I also remember the children at the school, and newborns and thousands of other joys.

Whenever I see curly blond hair, I remember the young woman who was killed by dogs, as well as the young man who came back from the dead. Neither powerful story reflects the whole color of life.

When I see pretty pink toenails, I recall the plane crash. I also am gladdened by these bright painted giggles of life, these tiny battle flags arrayed against the forces of darkness.

Light beats dark, but only by one letter. That is also true for alive beats dead, good beats bad and yes beats no. On balance, ignoring the good possibility of a God making all this right, I conclude that it is all worth it, for everyone. (Exceptions may apply, but you can't make assumptions.) My life in the ED has brought me joy and pain, in almost equal balance, but I wouldn't really trade it for . . . for what? It's my life, the only one I've got.

It's *all* a matter of Life and Death. The only life anyone has is their own and there is an expiration date, so make sure you don't fight any unnecessary fights, be careful with flammable liquids, wear your seatbelt, don't play with guns, wear your safety goggles, do not drink lye, do not waste time acting sick if you are not, keep your bucket list up to date if you are going to ride a motorcycle, wear a helmet for whatever, avoid things that make you sick for minimal benefit (smoking), take your blood pressure medication, lose a few pounds, get off the couch, be a part of something, cherish those you love, etc.

Epilogue

(Please read this, all medical personnel, especially nurses)

Taking care of patients is definitely a team sport. Believe me, you do not want to go it alone. ED doctors are useless without a whole array of teammates. These battle buddies are all friends, some fairly close. I will miss someone crucial in this listing, but nurses, EMS, techs, x-ray, chaplains, educators, security, maintenance, social workers, registration, housekeeping and the occasional administrator are all absolutely essential. There are also respiratory, physical, speech and rehab terrorists . . . I did not misspell "therapists."

Why do I call these people "terrorists?" An example:

"Mrs. Smith, does it hurt you to move your arm?" the docile-appearing young female in green scrubs asks the sweet old lady. "Yes? Then MOVE IT!" Much pain and suffering are caused by these personnel.

Of course, there is untold suffering with all the IV sticking, chest-hair-pulling, bed bathing, catheterizing shenanigans that occur in the course of the patient interacting with Team Healthcare. OK, OK, you're right. This joke has gone on too long, and I will now stop joking.

All of this care I mention above is critical and, aside from the still-too-common error, the suffering caused by the Team pales in significance compared to the suffering relieved. We doctors and we patients all would be lost without this army of folks that actually provides the healing directly to the patient.

I must end this book, and my career, with a note about nurses. For my purposes, "nurses" needs some qualification. I have often stated my position that male nurses are highly trained, valued, and respected healthcare heroes. I have never stated that about female nurses, but they are not bothered by that. They know that I am just keeping my "schtick" in operating condition.

It doesn't mean I don't truly respect male nurses. They are tough, capable—the kind of guys you want with you in a bar fight. If the one with you is not the muscular type, he will still excel at treating any injuries you sustain while awaiting the ambulance. Male nurses endure a lot and give a lot. Many of them I count as friends.

These men are not machines. They feel and grieve. They are used up and beaten down by the system. They have to use the same tricks that I use to keep afloat and keep their souls.

There may be other categories of nurses hidden under scrubs, but I will only discuss one other category. The female nurses are in a different league than the males. Of course, my eye-rolling wife may think she knows why I would say that, and she is partly right, but there is more.

These women work in a different universe from us men. We can more readily compartmentalize or remain a little distant to the death or disease, but these women have to immerse themselves right in it.

I am mostly talking to nurses, because of my role proximity to them, but I also am including numerous other women caregivers in this category: RTs, x-ray techs, medical assistants, and whoever else I've forgotten. Female physicians also deserve a little more credit than us men (although all the school is easier for them since they are smarter on average).

I know red flags are raised here; I understand there are lots of exceptions. Lots of female healthcare workers are partial psychopaths like myself, but I have seen numerous times with my own eyes that the experience of ED life by these women is usually different from my own.

I am certainly not claiming any differences in quality of care, competence, or compassion; I am claiming that the work is harder on most of them (not the peds nurse with the jokes or any number of brutal charge nurses).

The females sob alone or cry openly in groups. They cry real tears while I have already moved on to the next patient or—lunch.

Female nurses are insulted, abused by patients. They are manipulated and used by the system. They scramble to cover each other for illness or child emergencies; much of ordinary life is a struggle for them. They even feed their babies at work by milking themselves. The break room is a modern dairy.

They get off in the morning after twelve hours of hard labor to stay up a little longer to dress and drive kids to school. They are working more than full time for their paying job as well as working full time for their young children or old parents. They *feel* the weight of life in a way I do not have to.

Much is said of sexism, and anything we can do to minimize it is necessary, but ultimately, Mother Nature herself is sexist. Delivering babies, being a mother, having emotional intelligence—those things make it harder on women in lots of ways.

I do not want to imply that the women nurses are weak. Far from it, and actually, I mean the opposite. Most of them are working with greater risk than I, from Covid-19 or assaults or broken hearts. They have to calculate risks to their children, born or unborn. Most of them are not as equipped as I am to detach, compartmentalize, switch gears.

Most of them do not have the same support from home that I have. For my entire career, with little effort on my part, the children are cared for and raised, the house made homey and inviting. Even my lunches are packed for me.

These women do the hard work in the ED, frequently against all their inclinations. They take more risks and take more punishment. They put their hearts on the line—and get them crushed. I am saying that they are the greater heroes by far than us detached men with our built-in risk-taking genes.

I once got security's attention when I frightened this nurse so badly, she alerted the department with a hideous scream. All I did was sneak up on her quietly and stand there. When she turned around, Poof! I was there. This same experienced nurse was taking care of a dying old man. As she was starting an IV, he reached up and grabbed her breast. She tolerated the demented man's assault, finished her task and shrugged, "He's dying."

These women bring high-tech skills and otherworldly compassion to the most earthy places; these women pour themselves out for the worst of us, giving us their very souls. I have only one word for them and that word, spelled backwards, is "evol."

Acknowledgements

(This will be short, you shouldn't skip it)

Speaking of women, life would be awfully dull without those I have been married to. My wife has certainly been several different women, although her name hasn't changed, and her appearance hasn't changed much. I also reassure young men with this fact when they seem skeptical that you can be happily married to just one woman for decades: any one you marry will not be one woman for long.

Note: my wife's appearance hasn't changed much over the decades due to a huge collection of anti-aging concoctions. Although they have had some effect, if they really worked as advertised, she would be back in kindergarten.

I credit this multidimensional woman with dramatically improving my disposition as well as my effectiveness at work. Her tireless emotional and logistical support have been priceless.

I basically endured all the school and hard work to obtain and to keep her attention and to provide the best home I could for her and the children she bore.

I have loved all the women my wife has been and look forward, with some apprehension, to meeting my future wife. Her presence so far has helped me in every endeavor, and I expect this to continue (see "apprehension" above). I thank her with all my heart.

I also thank my children for being themselves and suffering from my child-rearing skills, certainly made worse by my Post Stress Stress Disorder. I hope they can heal from the damage I inflicted.

I would like to also thank my English Major wife for critiquing this book and finding lots of trivial and inconsequential mistakes I made, along with suggesting some improvements here and there. I suppose the reader should be more thankful.

I would like to thank my highly paid editor for finding even more problems: spelling errors (spelling shouldn't count), obscure and unnoticeable grammatical mistakes, or alleged stylistic mistakes. In addition, she also fixed everything and made me sound educated or at least sane and coherent. The reader should be particularly grateful to her.

I thanked coworkers in the epilogue above. I also need to thank all the thousands of patients who let me into their lives for those brief, but amazing glimpses at the human condition. Many of the stories in this book, told over the years to students and colleagues, have improved patient care through knowledge, or cheering up caregivers. For instance, dozens of students have been entertained by and have learned something very important from the woman whose mouth I set on fire. I thank her for her service. If she ever reads this book and recognizes her story (how could she not?), I will deny that I wrote this book that doesn't exist.

Jenny Linda
352 606 6160
6164
8/16 800 238-2727
9/2 2:40

Remick
503-216-1182

Made in United States
Orlando, FL
31 July 2022